American Torah Toons 2

Fifty-Four Illustrated Commentaries
by Lawrence Bush

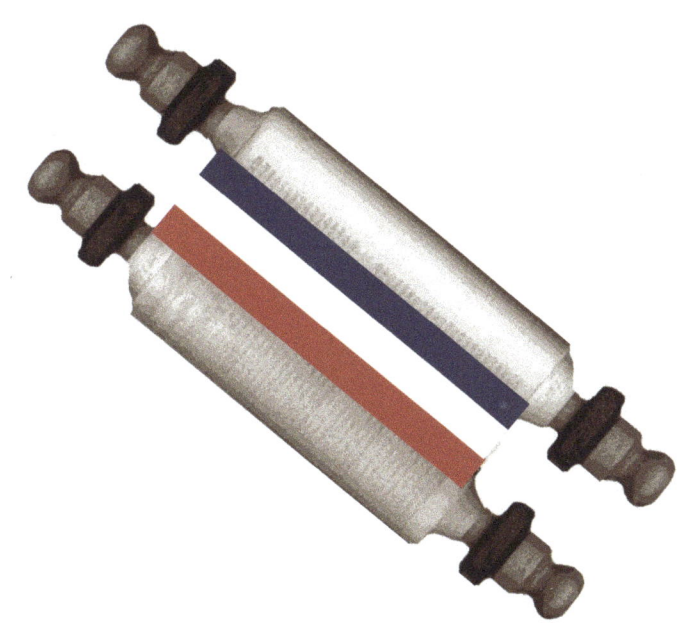

Ben Yehuda Press

American Torah Toons 2 ©2022 by Lawrence Bush. All rights reserved. No part of this book may be used or reproduced in any manner whatsoever without written permission except in the case of brief quotations embodied in critical articles and reviews.

Published by Ben Yehuda Press
122 Ayers Court #1B
Teaneck, NJ 07666

http://www.BenYehudaPress.com

To subscribe to our monthly book club and support independent Jewish publishing, visit https://www.patreon.com/BenYehudaPress

ISBN13 978-1-953829-26-9 paperback; ISBN: 978-1-953829-27-6 hardcover

For Zoë and Jonah

"Each child carries their own blessing into the world."
—Yiddish proverb

Introduction

In my decades as a writer and artist who works primarily with Jewish themes, I have often fallen into the cracks between the religious and the non-religious.

For that large plurality of Jews who "believe" and "observe," many of them passionately interested in Jewish texts and traditions, my self-identification as a "reluctant atheist" (in the subtitle of my book, *Waiting for God*) may seem bewildering, even offensive, while my universalist approach to Judaism — treating it less as the religious calling of a particular people than as a wisdom tradition for shaping compassionate human beings — seems idiosyncratic, at best.

For that large plurality of Jews who are non-religious, many of them ignorant about Judaism beyond a few of its holidays, my interest in Jewish themes, including religious themes, has marked me as an outlier, a provincial in our cosmopolitan world.

Nevertheless, *hineni*, here I am, still creating Torah toons, artworks that grapple with the first five books of the Hebrew Bible: Genesis, Exodus, Leviticus, Numbers, and Deuteronomy.

Why involve myself with the Torah this way? Why, especially, when I find its central character, Yood-Hey-Vov-Hey, also known as "the Lord your God," to be insufferable: dictatorial, patriarchal, obsessed with loyalty, obnoxiously vigilant about his public image, and downright ruthless? As portrayed in the Torah, the Lord your God is hardly a being I'd care to worship — or meet in a dark alley.

Now, some might argue that even an authoritarian deity is an improvement over the anarchic polytheism that seems to have dominated human culture before the invention of monotheism. In theory, at least, people living under the Lord your God, rather than constantly worrying about propitiating countless gods, have a clear, covenantal theology — *we'll do this if You do that* — which bespeaks a certain predictability and security in their lives. On the other hand, monotheism has provided ideological accompaniment to a great many conquests and crimes over the centuries, which certainly calls into question the idea of its being an evolutionary advance over the worship of multiple gods.

Whichever way we resolve this "comparative religion" debate, it's safe to say that a modern sense of relative predictability and security in life has allowed many monotheists to lose their "fear of God" altogether and replace it with a theology of awe, wonder, and gratitude, one that recasts God less as a punitive tyrant than as a loving parent or simply a cheerleader. Sacred texts such as the Torah have also been demoted by scholarship from "infallible" and "given by God" to lesser status as human-made historical composites, woven from many strands from many centuries, and reflecting the moral strivings as well as the limited mental frameworks of their times. These developments have provided space for the likes of me to escape feeling oppressed by fundamentalism and to become involved with religious thought without surrendering my rationality. Rabbi Mordecai Kaplan, the founder of Reconstructionist Judaism, spoke for me well when he acknowledged over eight decades ago (in *The Meaning of God in Modern Jewish Religion,* 1937) that "specific laws of the Torah . . . have, for the most part, become inoperative" due to their "authoritarian morality." Still, Kaplan urged us to study Torah in a "candid yet reverential spirit" that upholds the text as "a means of revelation . . ."

Unfortunately, however, most believing Jews, in my experience, rather than balancing the candid with the reverential, pursue the latter with little of the former as they try to reconcile their hope for spiritual uplift with texts that are stubbornly authoritarian, misogynistic, and inadequate for our complex lives. Why do they do so? Perhaps because we are *not* all that secure. As Tevye the

Milkman says in the musical stage adaptation of Sholem Aleichem's best-known book: "Tradition! Without our traditions, our lives would be as shaky as . . . as a fiddler on the roof!" In order not to fall off our roofs, we sacrifice candor to reverence in most worship services — and in most of what I see written about the Torah.

Nevertheless (and luckily for Judaism's longevity), the most revered and enduring interpretive writings about the Torah, namely, the Talmud and various volumes of *midrash* (centuries-old stories that elaborate upon the Torah), do bring a significantly more humane perspective than the Lord your God would have tolerated. Whereas the Torah, for example, proposes gruesome capital punishment for over two dozen trangressions, the Talmud (*Makkot* 7a) declares, "A rabbinic court that executes once in seven years is destructive." In the same vein, many rabbinic stories about God's interactions with humanity emphasize Yood-Hey-Vov-Hey's mercy and love far more than His peevishness. The writers of these commentaries and tales seemed intent on bringing the Torah into better alignment with the evolving social consciousness of the Jewish people — but never do their works openly criticize the original text's "authoritarian morality" or Yood-Hey-Vov-Hey's irritating personality. Instead, candor submits to reverence.

In *American Torah Toons 2,* I seek to reverse that: to sidestep reverence and strive for candor, to sidestep tradition and strive for creativity. My method is to springboard from the Torah text — often quite far from it — into visual storytelling that responds to the Torah's themes but is unconcerned with making the text look infallible or even necessarily righteous. When a passage complements my sense of justice and morality, my toon celebrates it; when a passage seems barbaric to me, my toon says as much. It is our lives as human beings, rather than Judaism's myths, that I aim to treat as sacred in this book.

Still, the question remains: If I revere neither God nor the Torah, why make art about them? Why risk falling between the cracks again?

My key motivation is that I cherish the fact that my people, American Jews (not all, but a significant sector of leaders, activists, and troublemakers), have embodied ethical, moral, and political values that I hold dear. They have been disproportionately represented in the labor movement, the civil rights movement, the women's movement, the helping professions, the arts, the sciences; they have cultivated American democracy, social justice, and creativity with great passion and heart. Even in our archly conservative times, three quarters of American Jews vote Democratic in nearly every election, compared with fewer than fifty percent of other "white" people, suggesting that, although most Jews in our country are "white," they are much less loyal to the racial caste system that has polluted so much of America's political history. There are many historical and cultural reasons why this is so (and I've worked for many years to help keep it so), but I do believe that the seeds of Jewish liberalism are found deeply buried in the Torah, the prime text of Jewish culture.

So never mind its cartoonish God character! The Torah's central story is about a people who are enslaved, gain their liberation, and are molded into a morally aware community. This story has shaped the passion for social justice for generations, and continues to inspire mine.

I've also always been consistently moved by the progression of the Torah from individuals to tribes to a nation — from a family to the world — which recapitulates our own psychological evolution from childhood to adulthood. And I've found the Torah's specific teachings about economic justice, and its innovative ideas that human beings are at our best when we are aware of ourselves as an interdependent community — and that we require the discipline of law and a sense of covenant to cultivate that awareness — to be brilliant and true. All of this compels my interest in making artworks based on the Torah.

The format of *American Torah Toons 2* limits itself to mere slivers of Torah text, with one artwork for each of the Torah's fifty-four "portions." As a result, my book reflects only bits and pieces of the

Torah's continuity, and can fruitfully be read at random.

There is a paragraph of commentary below each Torah passage, meant to set the stage for the toon. These brief commentaries include quotations or paraphrases from the Talmud and other venerable sources that I've taken primarily from *The Book of Legends,* H.N. Bialik and Y.H. Ravnitzky's classic encyclopedia of Talmud and Midrash, originally published in 1908-11 and republished by Schocken Books in 1992 (in translation by William Braude). The collages themselves are nearly all based on my own photographs, with some sampling of images that are in wide circulation. As for the numeral in the title, it's there because I produced a previous volume of *American Torah Toons*, in glorious black and white, published twenty-five years ago by Jason Aronson Books.

As I step again into the cracks — or perhaps, this time, over them — I want to thank you for taking the time to sit with my work, when there are so many other voices in this *meshugene* world calling for your attention.

Lawrence Bush
Accord, New York

GENESIS

BREYSHEET/In the Beginning *Genesis 1 to 6:8*

1:1-5 When God began to create Heaven and Earth — the Earth being unformed and void, with darkness over the surface of the deep and a wind from God sweeping over the water — God said, "Let there be light"; and there was light. God saw that the light was good, and God separated the light from the darkness. God called the light Day, and the darkness Night. And there was evening and there was morning, a first day.

This very first portion of the Torah raises questions about how "God" is to be named. In the Hebrew text, "Elohim" is used for the deity who creates the universe, but when human beings appear in Genesis 1:26, God is designated as "Yood-Hey-Vov-Hey" (YHVH), a.k.a. "Yahweh" or "Adonai." Some Talmudic interpreters considered "Elohim" to denote the divine attribute of justice, and "YHVH" the divine attribute of mercy. Rabbi Harold Schulweis, trying to reconcile belief in the Almighty's goodness with the reality of human suffering, wrote that "Elohim" represents the "world of is," while "YHVH" represents the "world of ought." "'Elohim,'" Schulweis suggested, "is revealed in the raw materals, 'Adonai' in the transformation that is enabled through the collaboration of the human."

Quotation Marks

Maimonides believed in a God so incomprehensible that all we can describe is what God is not.

The kabbalists believed that God is both transcendent and immanent, limitless and manifest.

Me, I don't believe in God — at least not a God with whom I could have a meaningful conversation.

Yet I do recognize the God-feeling, and the usefulness of God-language as a tidy way to express my amazement...

... at the fact that light travels at 186,000 miles per second! — and nothing can travel faster!

... that the Sun burns and the Earth turns, and night becomes day becomes night.

... that my very own body has thirty trillion cells, each a tiny factory of life!

... that I have food to eat, a house to live in, a car to drive, and all that, because of human effort around the globe for centuries.

Et cetera. We lead a miraculous existence!

So maybe, if we were simply to surround that word, "God," with quotation marks, we could all be happy — Maimonides, the kabbalists, and I.

NOAKH/Noah *Genesis 6:9 to 11*

9:22-27 Ham, the father of Canaan, saw his father's nakedness and told his brothers … When Noah woke up from his wine and learned what his youngest son had done to him, he said, "Cursed be Canaan/The lowest of slaves/Shall he be to his brothers." And he said, "Blessed be the LORD/the God of Shem/ Let Canaan be a slave to them./May God enlarge Japheth/And let him dwell in the tents of Shem/ And let Canaan be a slave to them."

This scene takes place after the Flood has wiped out nearly all life on Earth, and Noah, a survivor, has planted a vineyard and gotten drunk. The passage is sometimes called "the Curse of Ham," although it is actually Ham's son Canaan who is being cursed, despite his being innocent of any misdeed, "The Curse of Ham" was invoked throughout American history as "proof" that African people were meant by "God" to be enslaved. As recently as the 1960s, Southern segregationists were citing it to condone their racist policies, and even half a century after American apartheid was abolished, some evangelical Christian leaders were still invoking the Curse to explain their tolerance for white supremacist politics.

While Ham's descendants, according to the Torah's genealogy, included Ethiopians and Egyptians, most enslaved Africans in the Americas came from western Africa. Geography, however, like most other facts, has little bearing upon the theorizing of racists.

Chicago Blues

I got the Curse of Ham,
O yes I do,
because I saw my country naked,
saw its evil ways, too.

O Lord Above,
how long must I carry these blues?

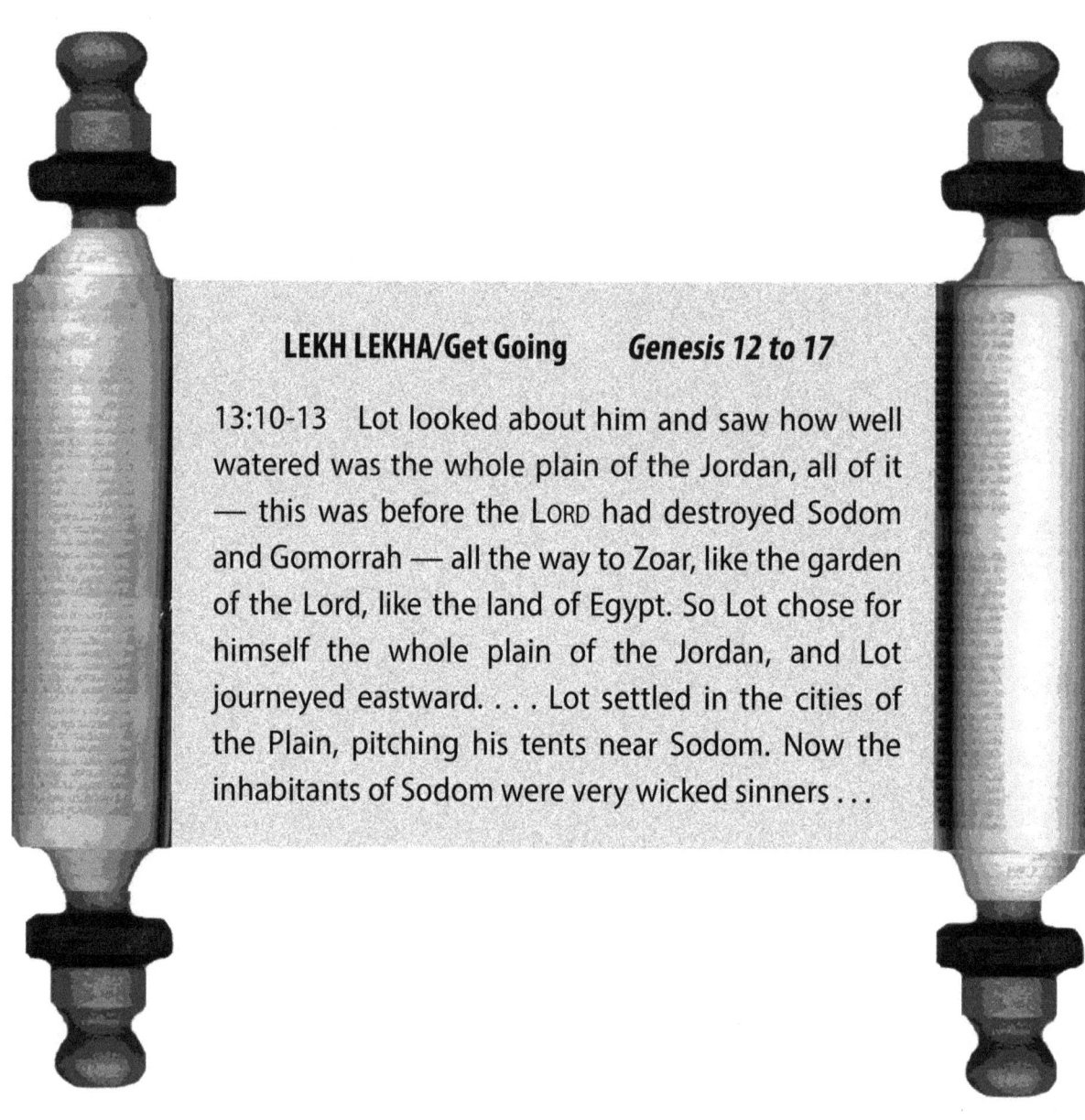

LEKH LEKHA/Get Going   *Genesis 12 to 17*

13:10-13 Lot looked about him and saw how well watered was the whole plain of the Jordan, all of it — this was before the Lord had destroyed Sodom and Gomorrah — all the way to Zoar, like the garden of the Lord, like the land of Egypt. So Lot chose for himself the whole plain of the Jordan, and Lot journeyed eastward. . . . Lot settled in the cities of the Plain, pitching his tents near Sodom. Now the inhabitants of Sodom were very wicked sinners . . .

While the Torah identifies residents of Sodom with a mob of rapists, the Talmud elaborates that the city's sins had to do with its prosperity, as witnessed by Lot in the above passage from "Lekh Lekha." Their fertile land and their easy wealth, rather than fostering gratitude and generosity, produced greed, cruelty, and mistreatment of wayfarers, the poor, and the vulnerable.

The Outrage of Sodom

Our Masters taught: The people of Sodom were arrogant because of their great wealth. They said: We live in peace and plenty — food can be got from our land, gold and silver can be mined from our land, precious stones and pearls can be obtained from our land. What need have we to look after wayfarers, who come to us only to deprive us? Come, let us see to it that the duty of hospitality be forgotten in our land. —based on Talmud, Sanhedrin 109b

VAYEIRA/And God Appeared *Genesis 18:1 to 22:24*

22:9-11   They arrived at the place of which God had told him. Abraham built an altar there; he laid out the wood; he bound his son Isaac; he laid him on top of the altar, on top of the wood. And Abraham picked up the knife to slay his son. Then an angel of the Lord called to him from heaven: "Abraham! Abraham!" And he answered, "Here I am."

The Akedah, or Binding of Isaac, portrays a human sacrifice that is commanded by "God" as a test of faithful obedience, then averted by a last-minute heavenly intervention. It is one of several scenes in the Torah that led the Talmudic rabbis to teach that justice without mercy can lead to the destruction of the world.

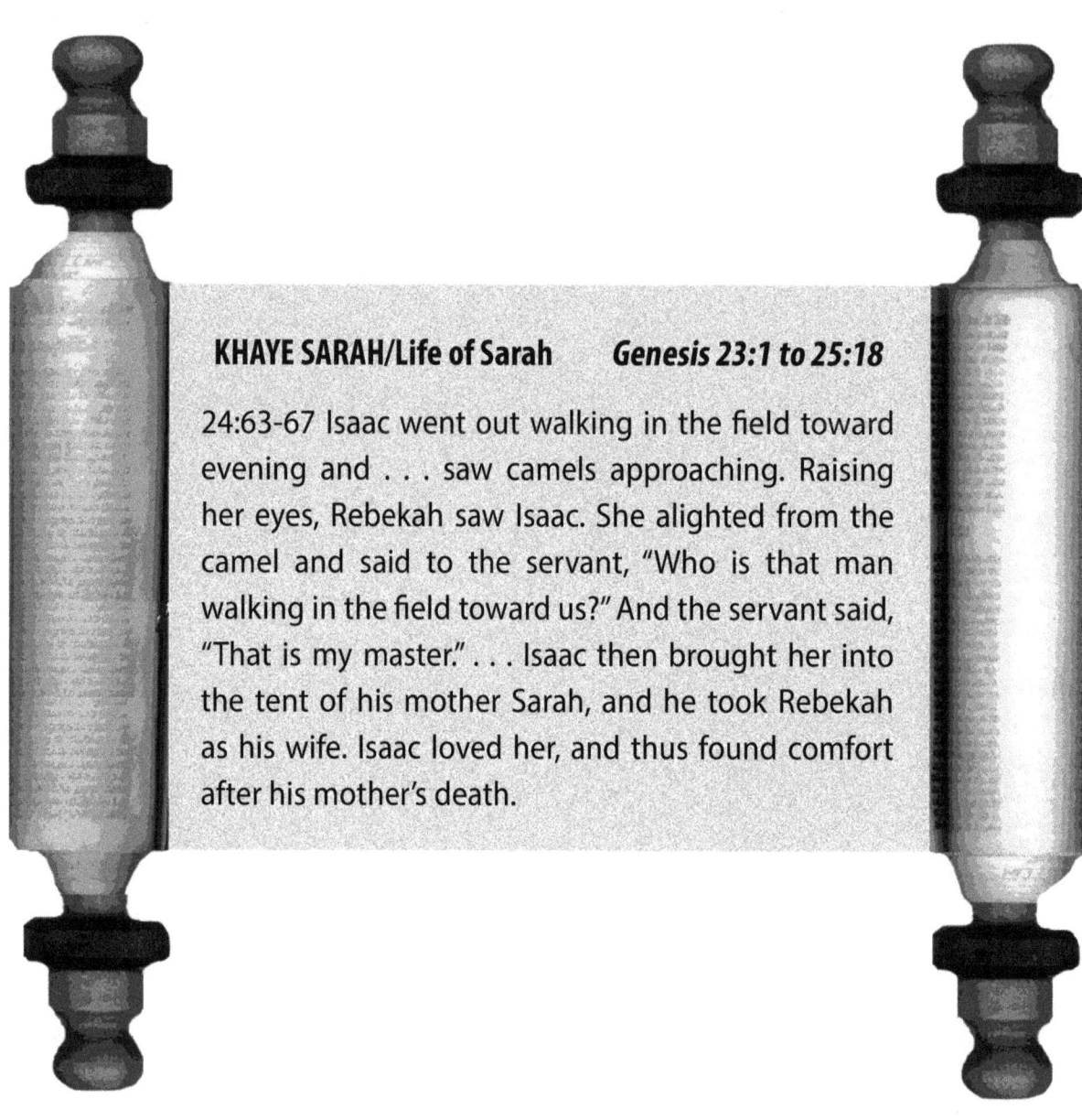

KHAYE SARAH/Life of Sarah   *Genesis 23:1 to 25:18*

24:63-67 Isaac went out walking in the field toward evening and . . . saw camels approaching. Raising her eyes, Rebekah saw Isaac. She alighted from the camel and said to the servant, "Who is that man walking in the field toward us?" And the servant said, "That is my master." . . . Isaac then brought her into the tent of his mother Sarah, and he took Rebekah as his wife. Isaac loved her, and thus found comfort after his mother's death.

"When Rebekah came" to Isaac, the son of Abraham and Sarah, "openness returned," says *Genesis Rabbah*, a key collection of *midrashim* (rabbinic stories that elaborate on Torah passages). ". . . When Rebekah came, the blessing returned . . . when Rebekah came, the light returned."

Grand Canyon

Her black braid, her flowered halter-top, as she kneels to unchain her red bicycle on a hot summer day. I've seen her on this block before, here and all around the neighborhood. I've even worked alongside her for a couple of hours with the toddlers at Liberation Nursery. So I pull the squirt gun from my pocket (standard nursery equipment) and she goes eek! and her red bike springs a flat tire. ※ We fall asleep at 1 a.m., her head on my shoulder. We wake up at 8 a.m. and her head's still there. ○ We hitchhike across America, unscathed, for nine weeks during the summer of Patty Hearst. By the time we reach San Francisco, we can recount 110 rides. ※ We hike to the bottom of the Grand Canyon and out in four days. ○ We share a bed, a refrigerator, a bathroom, a front door, and grow corn and watermelon in our backyard in Brooklyn. ※ We officiate at our own wedding. ○ She spends all our gift money to mount a dance production. ※ We have made love 700 times and still want to. ○ We bury my father. ※ We hold hands in London, Paris, Nice, Rome, Florence, Venice, Amsterdam, Nairobi, Toronto, Moose Jaw, Tel Aviv, Copenhagen, Ljubljana, New Delhi, New Orleans. ○ We advertise for babies in the Oneida Pennysaver, score with twins. ※ She has two back surgeries. I lose my gall bladder. ○ We try an open marriage for ten unhappy months. ※ We visit our children in summer camp and can't keep our hands off each other on the way home. ○ I resolve never to say no when she asks me to dance. ※ We hike with our kids to the bottom of the Grand Canyon and out in four days. ○ She organizes twelve friends to buy me a 12-string guitar. ※ We bury her father. ○ We hear the 17-year cicada for the third time. ※ We celebrate our daughter's marriage. ○ We have made love 4,000 times and still want to. ※ We bury our thirteenth cat and our fourth dog. ○ We pay off our mortgage. ※ We bury my mother. ○ She learns to play bass guitar and we form a duo. ※ We bury her mother. ○ She gets a Fulbright and takes me to India. ※ We meet our first grandchild. ○ We both retire. ※ We celebrate our son's marriage. ○ I publish my thirteenth and last book. ※ We take our grandchildren to what's left of the Pacific Redwoods. ○ I die while resting after a squirt-gun fight with her. ※ She dies during a dream about making love in the Grand Canyon with the full moon lighting up the walls.

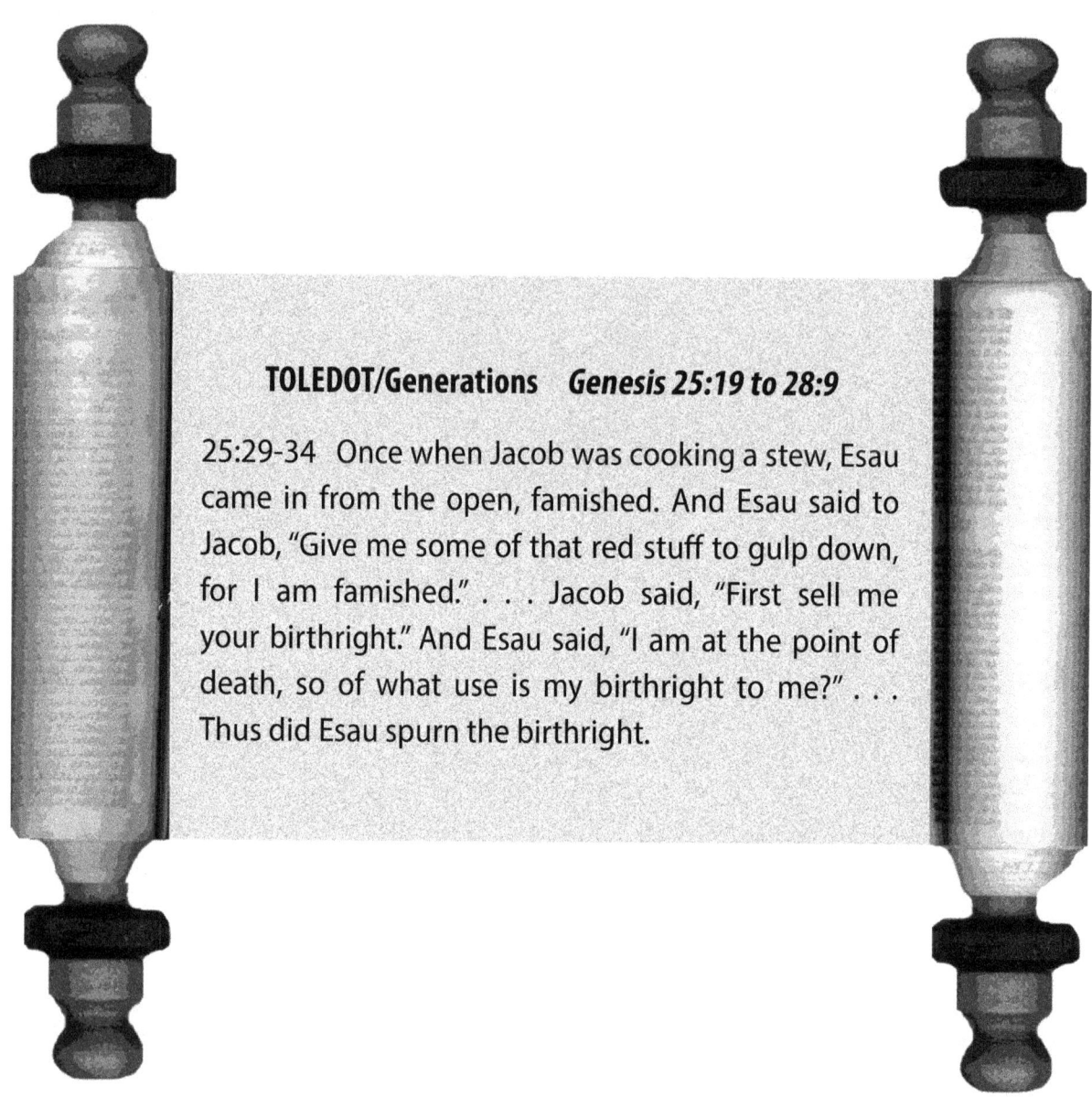

TOLEDOT/Generations *Genesis 25:19 to 28:9*

25:29-34 Once when Jacob was cooking a stew, Esau came in from the open, famished. And Esau said to Jacob, "Give me some of that red stuff to gulp down, for I am famished." . . . Jacob said, "First sell me your birthright." And Esau said, "I am at the point of death, so of what use is my birthright to me?" . . . Thus did Esau spurn the birthright.

In a kind of Biblical Cold War, twin brothers Jacob and Esau struggle for dominance over one another even in their mother Rebekah's womb. Many commentators observe that when Esau spurns his birthright for a bowl of stew, he is revealing his unfitness to lead the people who will become the Jews. Jacob, by contrast, although he begins his adulthood by cheating his brother, will enter deeper and deeper into spiritual introspection and eventually emerge, humbled and renamed, as "Israel."

BIRTHRIGHT

I grew up as a red-diaper baby: against capitalism and religion, against war and racism, and hopeful about the empowerment of the human collective, i.e., socialism.

My parents also taught me to be a skeptic, to question all "given wisdom."

The main thing that I ended up questioning was the empowerment of the human collective, i.e., socialism. Now, where's that bowl of stew?

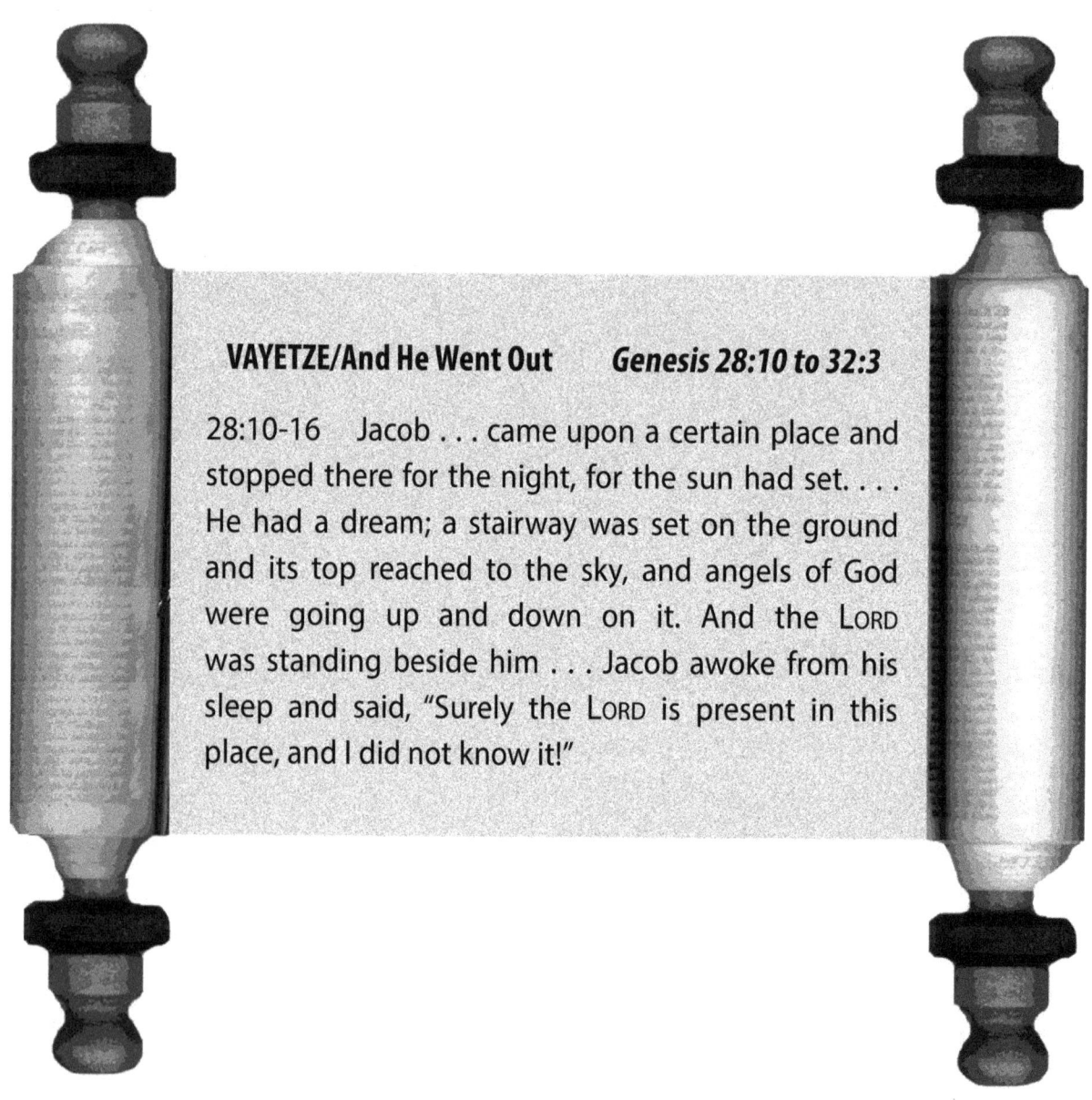

VAYETZE/And He Went Out   *Genesis 28:10 to 32:3*

28:10-16   Jacob . . . came upon a certain place and stopped there for the night, for the sun had set. . . . He had a dream; a stairway was set on the ground and its top reached to the sky, and angels of God were going up and down on it. And the Lord was standing beside him . . . Jacob awoke from his sleep and said, "Surely the Lord is present in this place, and I did not know it!"

"Dreams," writes Eric Fromm, "are like a microscope through which we look at the hidden occurrences in our soul."

"Dreams," says *Genesis Rabbah*, "are the incomplete form of prophecy."

Dreams

After seven decades of life, I often recall dream imagery from my childhood with more detail and intensity than I recall about real events —

. . . the tiny horses that I discovered and joyously rode up and down the block . . .

. . . knowing how to fly but being unable to gain altitude above people's knees, until I learned to arch my back and RISE . . .

. . . the endlessly roomy mansion that I swear, to this day, I actually visited . . .

. . . the man I killed in self-defense, and then I killed others to avoid arrest, all the while thinking, *I'm sorry, it didn't have to be this way, can't we reverse time?*

. . . the white doves that circled my head, then splattered into the building, dropped to the ground, and resurrected as white Great Danes that walked majestically at my side . . .

But in my third decade, my wife-to-be Susan commandeered my dream life:

. . . the surreptitious call to my old girlfriend — *rrring! rrrring! rrring!* — and as soon as she says, "Hello?" my apartment goes dark. I've been cut off by the electric company!

. . . the evening of house parties, one after another, in which I keep scanning people's bookshelves and cabinets for *Playboy* magazines — never finding one, and each time looking over at Susan, who is patiently waiting for me . . .

. . . the visit from my dead father, who keeps asking to meet Susan . . .

"Surely my LOVE is present in this place, and I did not know it!"

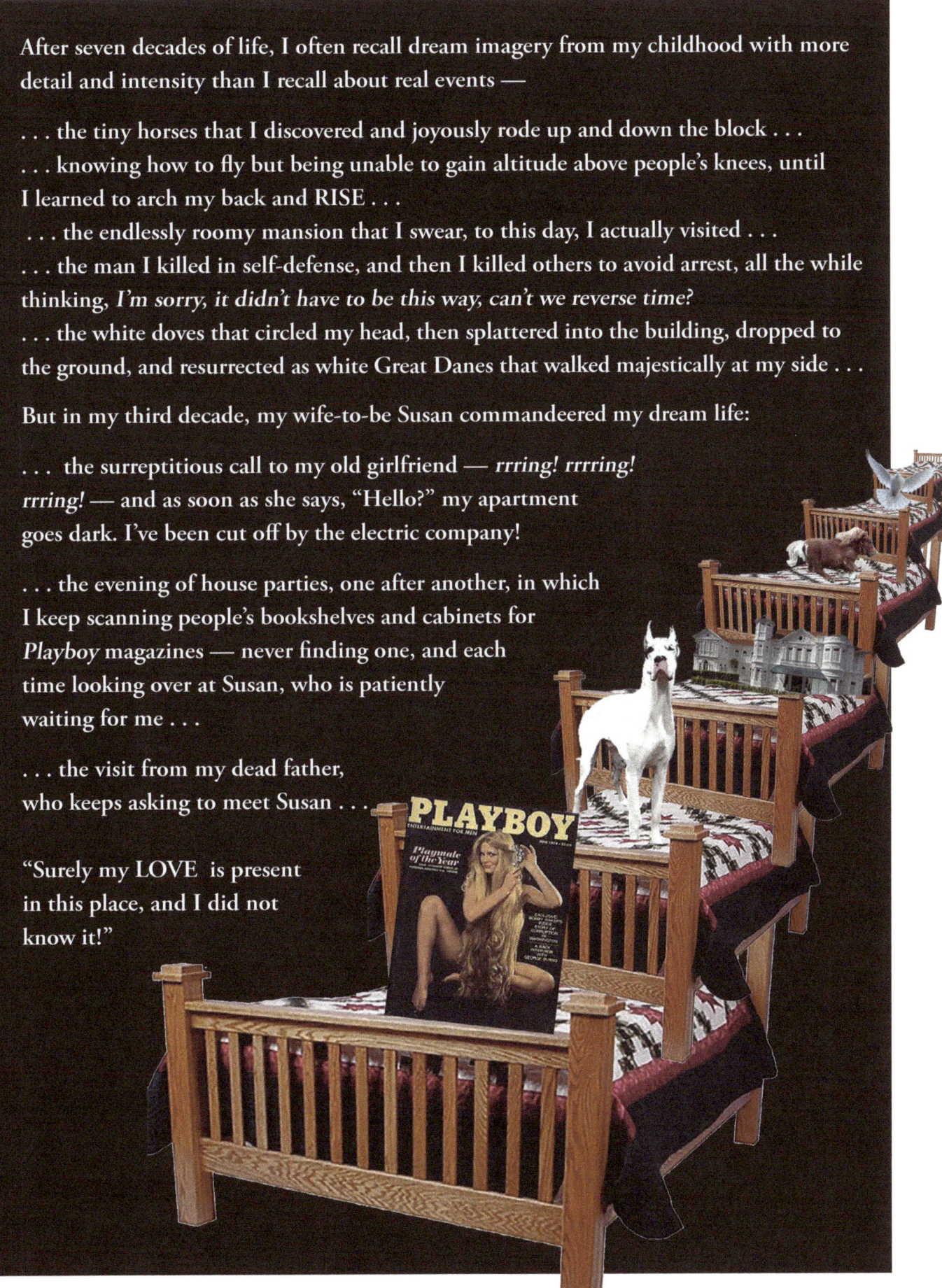

VAYISHLAKH/And He Sent   *Genesis 32:4 to 36:43*

32:25-32 Jacob was left alone. And a man wrestled with him until the break of dawn. When . . . [the man] had not prevailed against him, he wrenched Jacob's hip at the socket . . . Then he said, "Let me go, for dawn is breaking." But [Jacob] answered, "I will not let you go, unless you bless me." . . . Said he, "Your name shall no longer be Jacob, but Israel, for you have striven with beings divine and human . . ." The sun rose . . . as he passed Penuel, limping . . .

Throughout his life, Jacob seems blessed by "God" yet pursued by some other vengeful force for stealing his father's blessing from Esau. Fate has it that Jacob will prosper, but not before his future father-in-law, Laban, hoodwinks him into laboring for seven years, and then seven more, to earn his beloved Rachel as his wife. Laban then tries to cheat Jacob of his years of earnings, but "God" thwarts the effort.

It's not until Jacob wrestles with a mystical being, on the eve of a potentially deadly reunion with Esau, that he is sufficiently humbled and transformed from a prideful cad into a worthy leader.

A Song of Ascent

I used to be ambitious,
striving to be noticed
and admired.
Of all my secret wishes,
this was the one I trained for
all my life.

Now I just want to love you, my friends,
as best as I can, every day.
Now I just want to love you, my friends,
as best as I can.

Took pride in feeling handsome,
as if that made me special,
or mattered at all.
Took pride in feeling brilliant —
the only brilliant thing I know is
pride goes before a fall.

Now I just want to belong to a world
with good people sharing righteous ways,
and I can join in and love you, my friends,
as best as I can.

Oh, it took so long
to settle in, to belong.
Oh, I suffered so,
trying to be special.

I used to be so jealous
of every man who
rose above the crowd.
But now I tell you, fellas,
I'd rather be right here with you,
laughing out loud.

All I really want is to love you, my friends,
as best as I can, every day.
All I really want is to love you, my friends,
as best as I can.

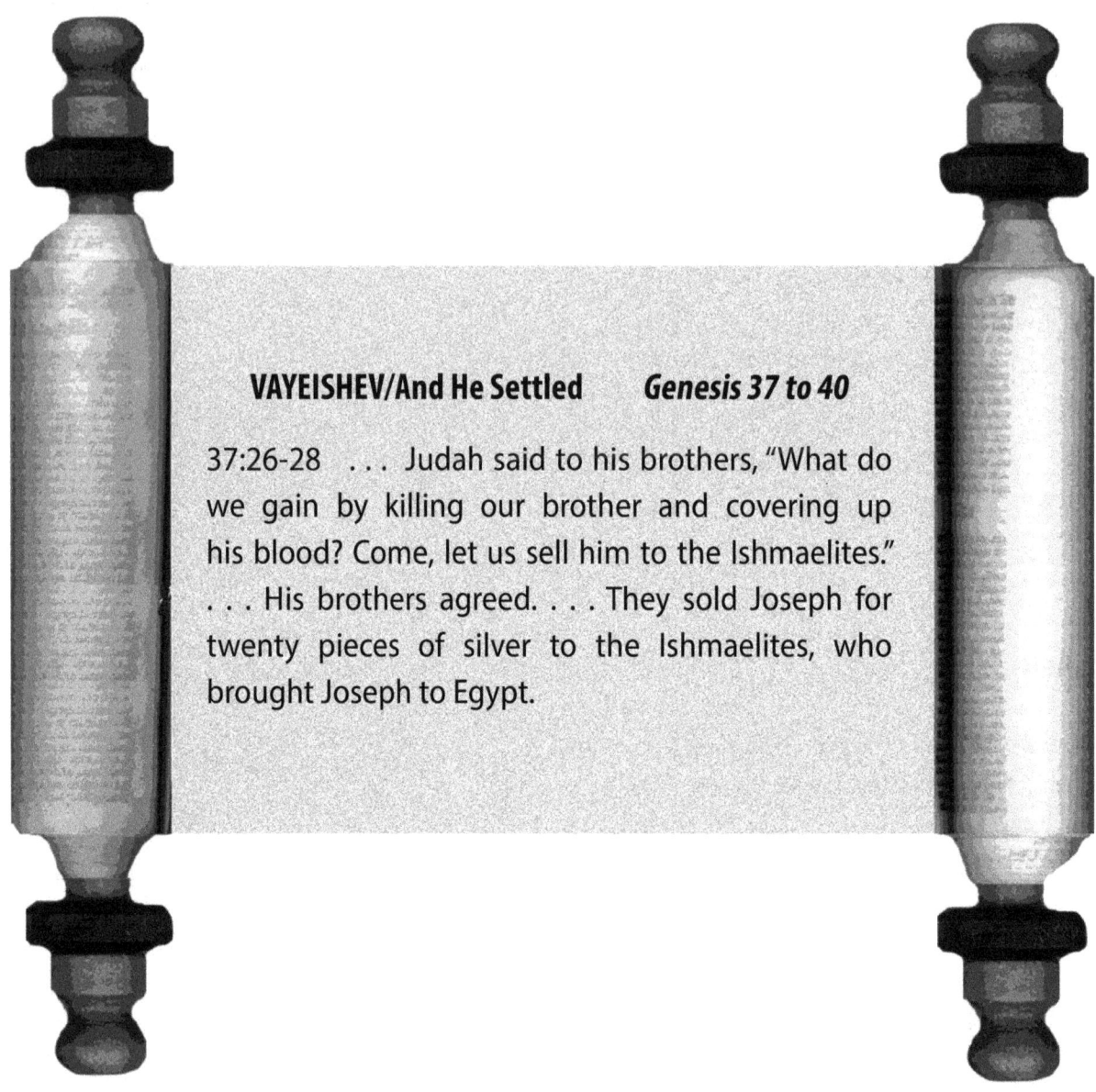

VAYEISHEV/And He Settled   Genesis 37 to 40

37:26-28 . . . Judah said to his brothers, "What do we gain by killing our brother and covering up his blood? Come, let us sell him to the Ishmaelites." . . . His brothers agreed. . . . They sold Joseph for twenty pieces of silver to the Ishmaelites, who brought Joseph to Egypt.

The Torah assigns more than four centuries of enslavement in Egypt to the Israelites, beginning with Joseph's betrayal by his brothers. When liberation comes, the Midrash portrays "God" as healing the ex-slaves: "Because of their servitude in clay and bricks, My children's look of good health has not yet come back . . . Let My children be indulged for two or three months — with the manna, with the waters of the well, with the quail — then I will give them the Torah" (*Ecclesiastes Rabbah* and *Song of Songs Rabbah*).

Greed and inhumanity produced two and a half centuries of enslavement in America to captured Africans and their descendants, followed by another century and a half of betrayal, segregation, terroristic lynching, and endless discrimination. When will manna, waters of the well, and quail at last be offered to them and their children?

MIKETZ/At the End   *Genesis 41 to 44:17*

43:26-28 When Joseph came . . . they presented to him the gifts that they had brought with them into the house, bowing low before him to the ground. He greeted them, and he said, "How is your aged father of whom you spoke? Is he still in good health?" They replied, "It is well with your servant our father; he is still in good health." And they bowed and made obeisance.

The once-enslaved Joseph has become the powerful prime minister of Egypt, and is steering the country through seven years of harsh famine. When the brothers who long ago betrayed and sold him into slavery arrive in Egypt as starving supplicants, Joseph bullies and terrifies them, but he is conscience-stricken while doing this, knowing that his long-afflicted father Jacob awaits their safe return.

Morrie

My father was a depressed, withholding man. The youngest by far of eight children, he seemed to feel bullied by life, and sought his revenge by withdrawing from it. When he came home from his job as a pharmacist, the rule was that my brother and I had to "keep out of his hair" for at least a half-hour. Once he was settled in, he usually had a book or magazine in front of his face and a haze of cigarette smoke around his head.

I left home when I was 17, but for years after, I had an abiding yen for my father's attention. One evening I phoned at a later-than-usual hour, and in the course of our conversation I took a risk by complaining that he always seemed to keep me at arm's distance.

Dad was shocked. "Why do you say that?" he said. "You're the one person I can complain to bitterly and you don't judge me for it."

I learned at that moment that for Morris Bush, bitter complaint was the main way of sharing intimacy, and sympathetic listening was experienced as love.

From then on, instead of yearning for my father's attention, I gave him more of mine, and we became very close for a decade before cancer sealed him off for good at age 70.

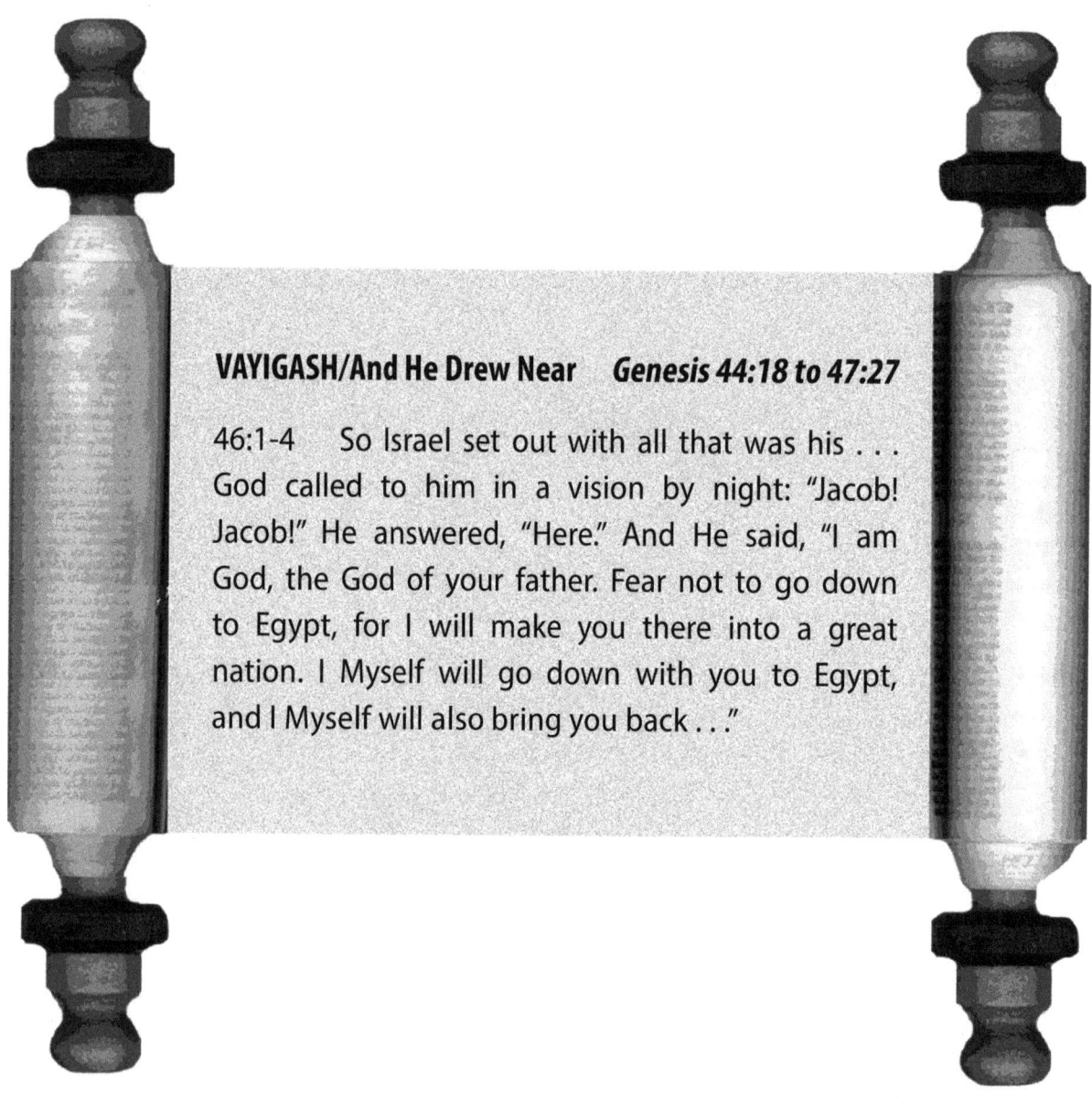

VAYIGASH/And He Drew Near *Genesis 44:18 to 47:27*

46:1-4 So Israel set out with all that was his . . . God called to him in a vision by night: "Jacob! Jacob!" He answered, "Here." And He said, "I am God, the God of your father. Fear not to go down to Egypt, for I will make you there into a great nation. I Myself will go down with you to Egypt, and I Myself will also bring you back . . ."

Even after reaching his spiritual maturity, Jacob a.k.a. Israel remains a fearful, calculating man. But "God" reassures him with promises that he will survive his ordeals to foster a great nation. This same "God" will subsequently repeat the command to members of that "great nation" to remember that they themselves experienced oppression and fear in Egypt and should therefore offer dignity, protection, respect and support to strangers, sojourners, and vulnerable people. Throughout history, however, other nations did not heed that command, and Jews were forced, like Jacob, to step into the fearful unknown, time and again.

Permission Granted

I used to work at home for so many hours that I became afraid to leave the house — afraid that I'd miss an email, an opportunity, a responsibility. I called myself a homebody, but I was really becoming an agoraphobe. So I asked Susan to see if, for my birthday, she could locate an old-fashioned ticket dispenser, the kind you might find at a crowded deli counter: You push the lever, you get a number, you wait your turn. She couldn't find one, so instead she made me a "Permission Box," which dispensed tickets. Each time I left the house, I would put a ticket into my wallet, and after about five times I didn't need to perform the ritual. The Permission Box. Every therapist should have one.

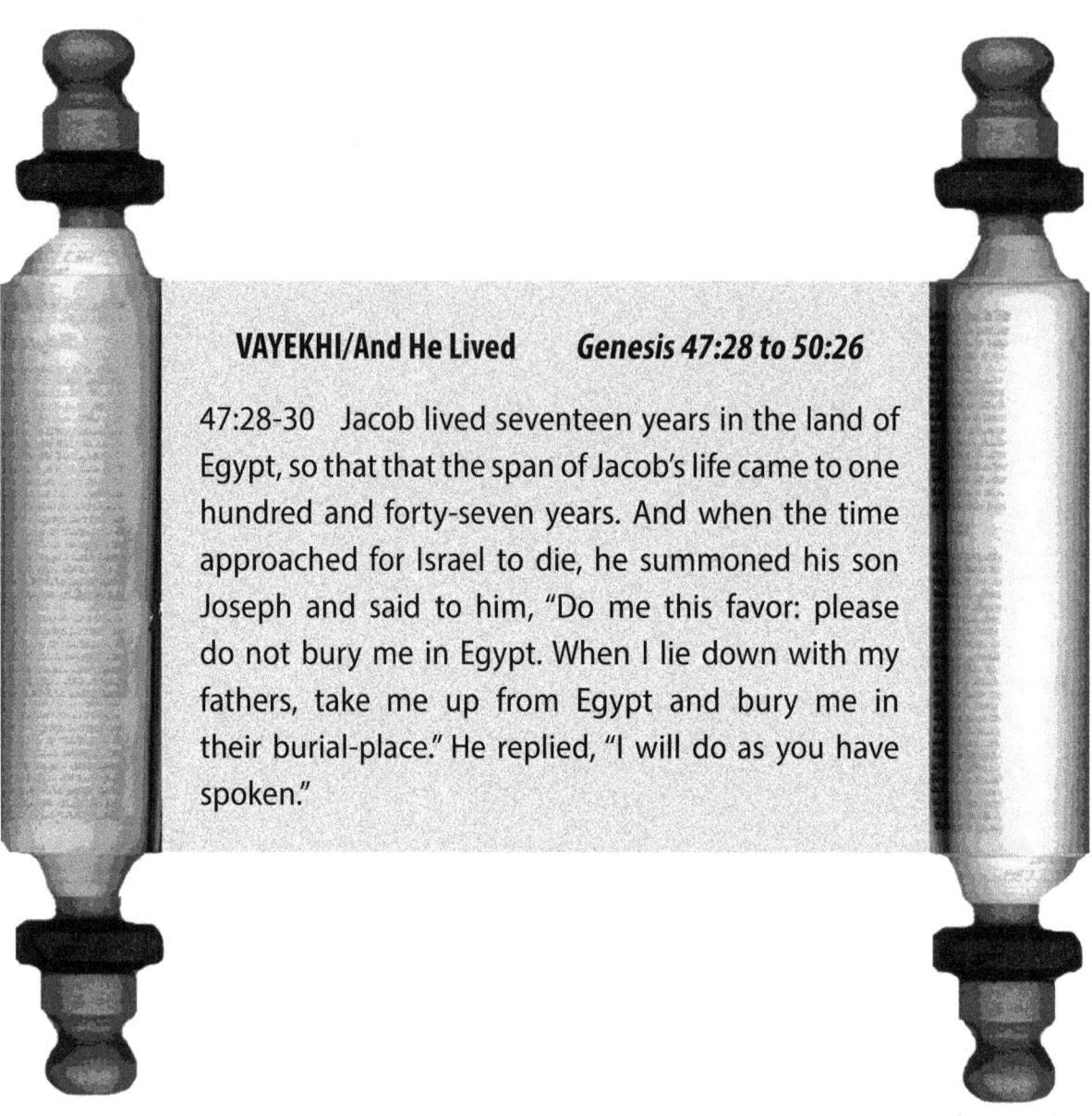

VAYEKHI/And He Lived *Genesis 47:28 to 50:26*

47:28-30 Jacob lived seventeen years in the land of Egypt, so that that the span of Jacob's life came to one hundred and forty-seven years. And when the time approached for Israel to die, he summoned his son Joseph and said to him, "Do me this favor: please do not bury me in Egypt. When I lie down with my fathers, take me up from Egypt and bury me in their burial-place." He replied, "I will do as you have spoken."

In this final portion of the book of Genesis, Jacob/Israel assembles his sons at his deathbed and passes judgment upon them with a variety of blessings and curses. His favorite son, Joseph, is named "the elect of his brothers" (Jacob clearly has learned very little about the pitfalls of playing favorites) and is given the evocative and mysterious "Blessings of the deep that couches below,/Blessings of the breast and womb."

With the passing of the last of the patriarchs and matriarchs — Abraham and Sarah, Isaac and Rebekah, and Jacob, Leah, and Rachel — the Torah is ready to expand its focus from the fate of a single family to the fate of a whole people.

BLESSINGS OF THE BREAST AND WOMB

My mom Jacki was ravenous for love and affection, which made her a difficult woman to have as a mother. Even as a grandma, she would compete with my kids for my attention. I still tried to be a dutiful son, but I always felt buttoned up tight in her presence.

Not so the workers at her assisted-living place. They would wash her, dress her, comb her hair, put on her lipstick, speak lovingly to her, and tell me what a grand, elegant lady she was. These women, traveling in from long distances, working for lousy wages, and suffering the indignities of racism and near-poverty on a daily basis, all seemed eager to teach me how to show love and generosity to my old mom. There were times I had to restrain myself from sinking to my knees in front of them, arms outstretched, and shouting, *Thank you!*

Their lessons slowly took hold. Two weeks before Mom died at 92, I joined her for dinner in the institution's dining room, instead of taking her out or having Chinese food delivered to her room. I also brought along a guitar and a special song that I'd learned for her: "Just in Time." It was a tune she used to sing to me as a kid, to my enormous embarrassment: "Just in time, I found you just in time . . ."

I serenaded the whole dining room during dessert, and Mom kvelled from all the attention it brought her. Two weeks later, she was gone.

25

EXODUS

SHEMOT/Names *Exodus 1:1 to 6:1*

1:8-14 A new king arose over Egypt who did not know Joseph. And he said to his people, "Look, the Israelite people are much too numerous for us. Let us deal shrewdly with them, so that they may not increase; otherwise . . . they may join our enemies in fighting against us and rise from the ground." . . . The Egyptians ruthlessly imposed upon the Israelites the various labors that they made them perform. Ruthlessly they made life bitter for them . . .

In this first portion of Exodus, a new king of Egypt enslaves the descendants of Jacob and his sons, who had emigrated to Egypt during the years of famine. The pharaoh next pursues genocidal policies by killing the first-born sons of all their families. While the word "genocide" was not coined until the Holocaust was underway (by Raphael Lemkin, a survivor who became an international lawyer), policies of ethnic extermination are ancient. The Torah itself (Deuteronomy 20:15-18) will present YHVH repeatedly commanding genocide against the inhabitants of Canaanite cities — "you shall not let a soul remain alive" — when they are conquered by the Israelites. This is a command, however, that *Midrash Tanhuma* (a medieval volume of stories) says Moses refused to obey, instead protesting, like Abraham regarding Sodom and Gomorrah, "Shall I slay the innocent with the guilty?"

35,000 Robert Cantors

The first important thing I recall watching on television was the Eichmann trial, in 1961.

At school, we'd spend time thinking up ways for him to be tortured.

There were thirty-three kids in our 4th-grade class, nearly all of them Jewish, including two Lindas and two Davids — but let's keep it simple and say there were thirty-three kids with thirty-three different names.

There would have to be 35,000 of each — 35,000 Becky Silvers (real cute and sparkly), 35,000 Arnie Glicksteins (a klutz), 35,000 Sandi Meislers (snooty, but I liked her), 35,000 Reba Shapiros (a brain), 35,000 Robert Cantors (my best friend) — 35,000 of each to come even close to the number of kids Eichmann arranged to be murdered in only four years.

String him up by the nuts!

Pierce his skin with six million pins!

Cart him around in a cage and let people do whatever they want to him!

And I knew that he never shed a tear, not even afterwards, because, like I told Robert, if the guy's heart had opened even a crack, he would've had to commit suicide!

VAYERA/And I Appeared   *Exodus 6:2 to 9:35*

7:3-5 . . . I will harden Pharaoh's heart, that I may multiply My signs and marvels in the land of Egypt. When Pharaoh does not heed you, I will lay My hand upon Egypt and deliver My ranks, My people the Israelites, from the land of Egypt with extraordinary chastisements. And the Egyptians shall know that I am the Lord, when I stretch out My hand over Egypt and bring out the Israelites from their midst.

The first six "extraordinary chastisements" — blood, frogs, lice, swarms of insects, animal pestilence, and heavy hail — punish the land of Egypt for its centuries of mistreatment of the Israelites. Each time a plague goes dormant, however, the King of the Nile denies what is happening and stubbornly betrays his promise to let go of the enslaved Israelites, until his own courtiers are warning him: "Are you not yet aware that Egypt is lost?"

King of Denial

O Man of Men! O Sophisticated Demi-God! O Builder of Great Walls!
Stormy Daniels should have paid You!
What woman on Earth would not desire to be touched, nay,
grabbed, by your soft, shapely hands?

O Leader without Peer! You say, and it is so. You deem, and it is done.
You tweet, and your words fly like arrows to the hearts of the Libtarded!
O Great Disrupter, let us conspire together against the Conspirators!
Let us fake out the Fakers! Let us make fun of the Chinese!
Let us inhale bleach, together!
O Don Donald! Your image is too brilliant — we must turn away or die!

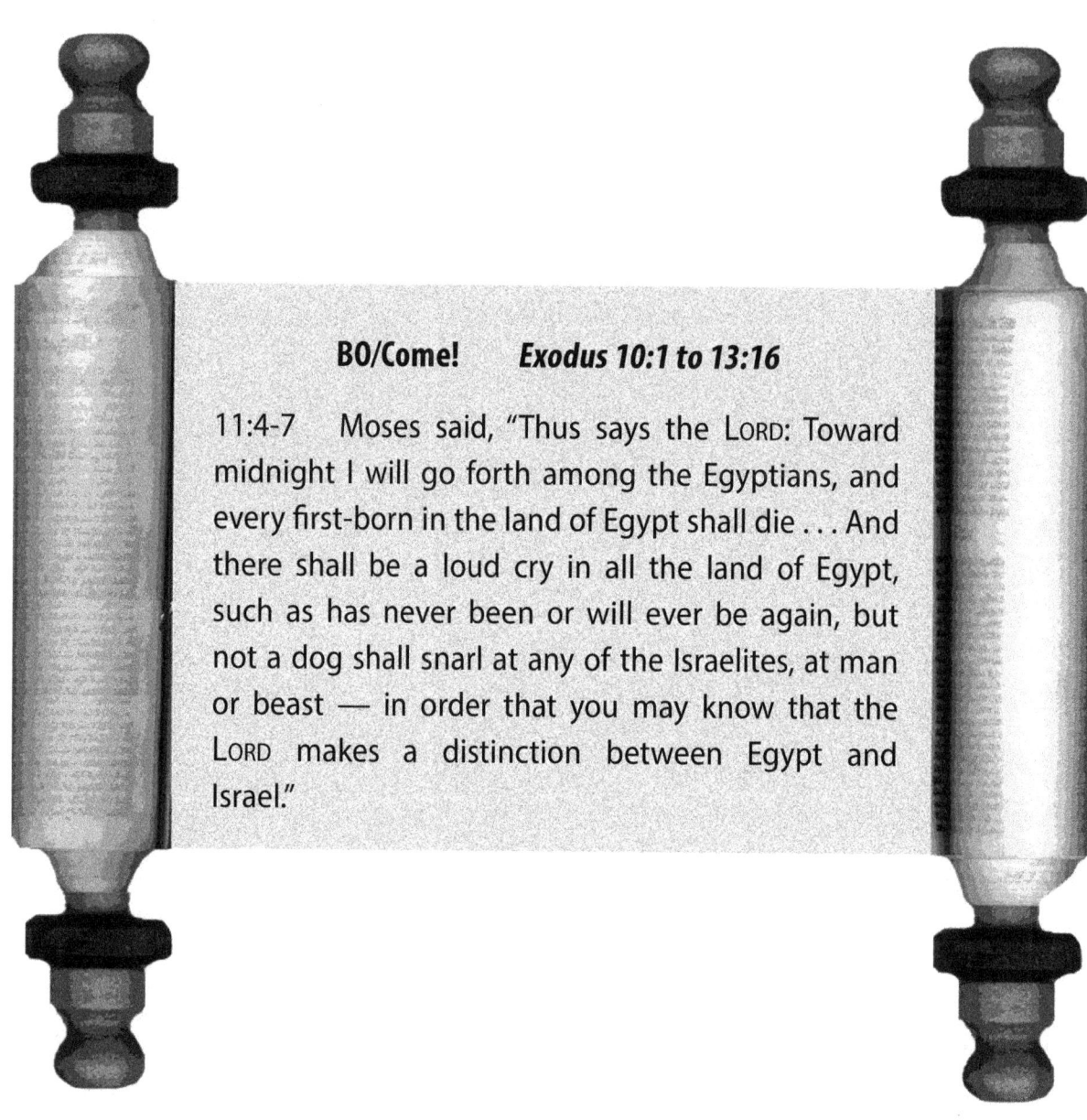

BO/Come!   *Exodus 10:1 to 13:16*

11:4-7   Moses said, "Thus says the Lord: Toward midnight I will go forth among the Egyptians, and every first-born in the land of Egypt shall die . . . And there shall be a loud cry in all the land of Egypt, such as has never been or will ever be again, but not a dog shall snarl at any of the Israelites, at man or beast — in order that you may know that the Lord makes a distinction between Egypt and Israel."

Pharaoh holds onto his power and his profits until the tenth and final plague strikes: The Angel of Death passes through Egypt and takes the lives of the first-born of every living thing except the Israelites, who are told in advance how to be safe in their houses (lamb's blood on the doorposts, etc.). Their descendants will celebrate this night as the festival of Passover.

Alas, there are no planetary doorposts to mark with blood so that the Angel of Death might pass over us all. As the classic Yiddish writer Y.L. Peretz wrote: "It is not only individuals — peoples, too, cannot merely live for themselves. The whole world must be redeemed."

Angel of Death

"Fools," he grumbled, "don't you see that the world is coming to its end?"

Whales! Elephants! Chimps! Mountain lions! Frogs, songbirds, bees, bugs!

BESHALAKH/When He Sent Out   *Exodus 13:17 to 17:16*

16:14-18   When the fall of dew lifted, there over the surface of the wilderness . . . lay a fine and flaky substance, as fine as frost on the ground. . . . And Moses said to them, "That is the bread which the Lord has given you to eat. . . . Gather as much of it as each of you requires . . ." The Israelites did so, some gathering much, some little. But when they measured it . . . he who had gathered much had no excess, and he who had gathered little had no deficiency . . .

The "manna from heaven," which feeds the Israelites in the wilderness for forty years, arrives daily and goes sour if hoarded or unconsumed. Talmudic commentators described it as tasting like different favorite foods to different people; as melting to form rivulets from which wildlife drank; and as teaching the people to have faith that their sustenance would be provided.

"Beshalakh" portrays Moses as commanding Aaron to "Take a jar, put one *omer* of manna in it, and place it before the Lord, to be kept throughout the ages." Perhaps in response, apothecary jars and other storage jars from the 19th and 20th centuries, including one that I inherited from my pharmacist father, sometimes boasted "manna" on their labels.

Sustenance

YITRO/Jethro   Exodus 18:1 to 20:23

20:15-17   All the people witnessed the thunder and lightning, the blare of the horn and the mountain smoking; and when the people saw it, they fell back . . . "You speak to us," they said to Moses, "and we will obey, but let not God speak to us, lest we die." Moses answered the people, "Be not afraid; for God has come only in order to test you, and in order that the fear of God may be ever with you, so that you do not go astray."

The "fear of God" is not often invoked as a motivating force in modern spirituality and theology — folks seem more into awe, gratitude, and joy than "Uh-oh, better watch my step" — but it is a major concern in the Torah. At Mount Sinai, after hearing the Ten Commandments from Moses' lips, the people stand back from a direct encounter with "God." Who can blame them? They are about to have rigors imposed upon their lives — dozens of regulations meant to restrict their appetites, their libidos, and their egos, and to yoke them together as a "God"-conscious, "God"-fearing community.

At a Distance

It was not a "bad trip" that ended my use of LSD when I was young. It was not the hallucinations, the intensity of sensual experience, the heebie-jeebies, the fragility of my ego, or the seeming weirdness of everything that's man-made.

I pretty much appreciated all that.

What scared me was the overwhelming intimation of interconnection — I saw it, strands of light connecting every living thing to every other living thing — and the terrible responsibility that reality would impose upon my life and my conscience were I to embrace it as real. That's what chased me away from Mount Sinai, back to the safety of my room.

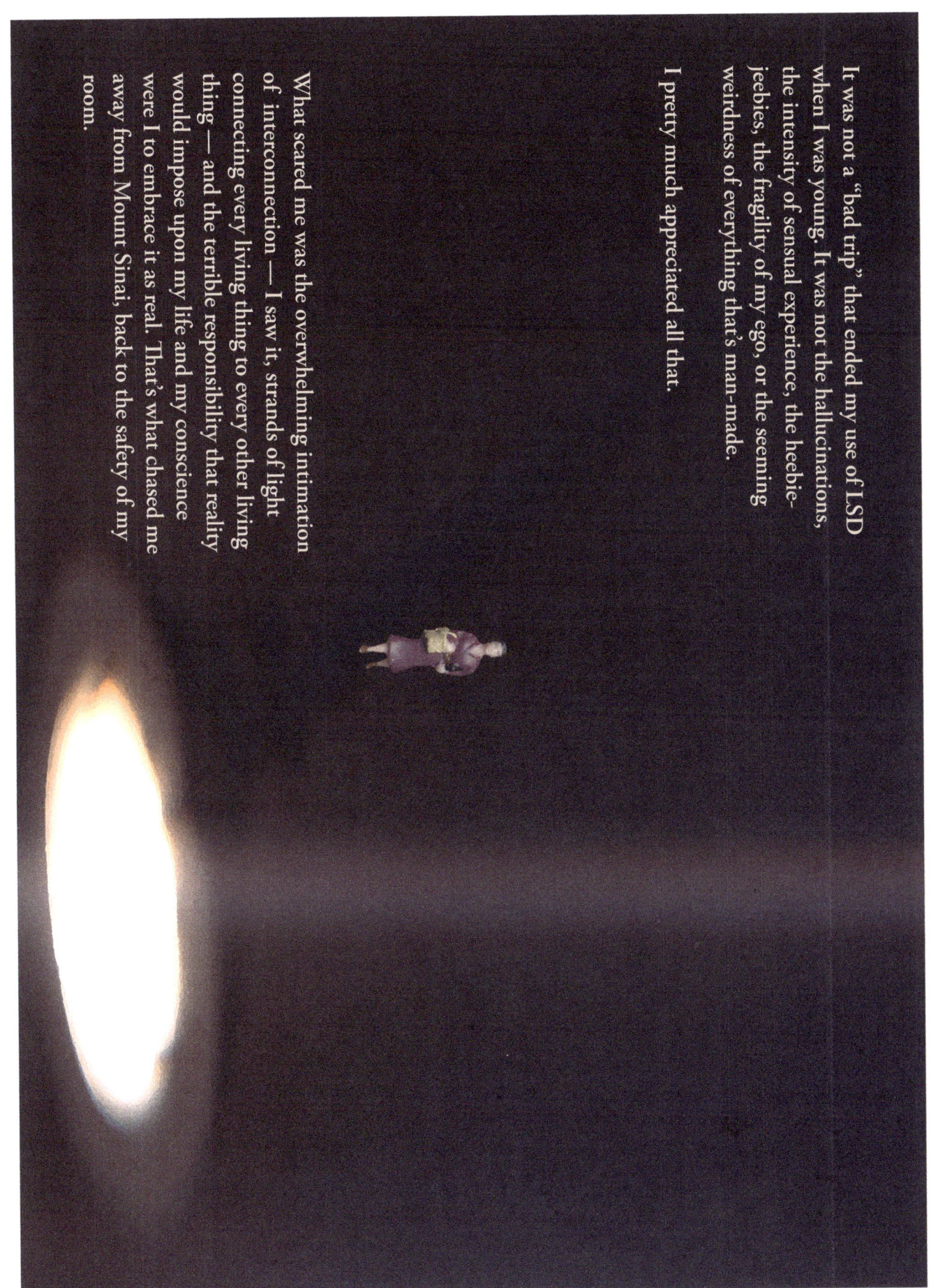

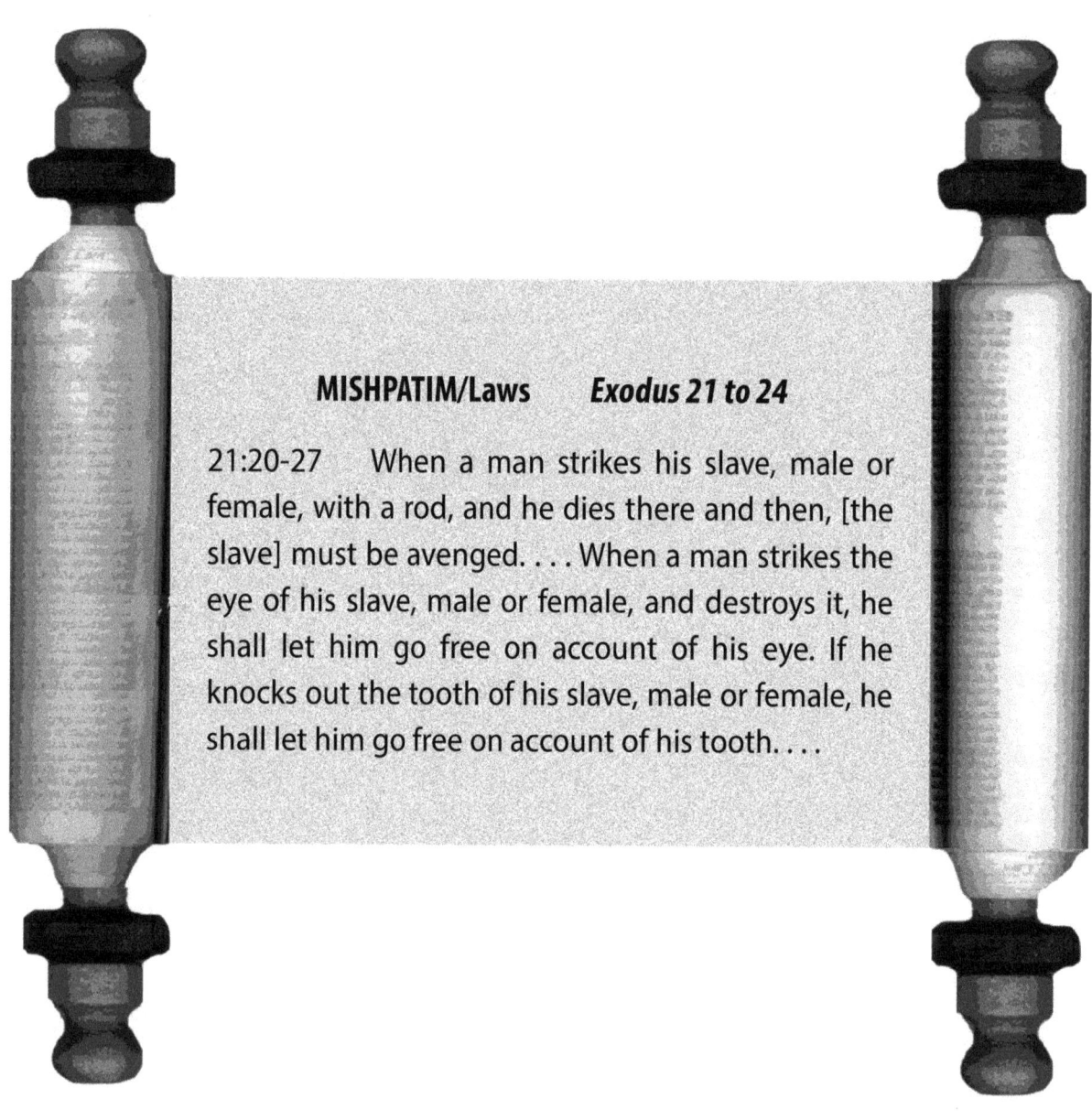

MISHPATIM/Laws   Exodus 21 to 24

21:20-27   When a man strikes his slave, male or female, with a rod, and he dies there and then, [the slave] must be avenged. . . . When a man strikes the eye of his slave, male or female, and destroys it, he shall let him go free on account of his eye. If he knocks out the tooth of his slave, male or female, he shall let him go free on account of his tooth. . . .

The Torah tolerates the enslavement of human beings but sets some limits on the exploitative power and arbitrary cruelty of slavemasters. These limits were very much ignored by most slavemasters in the USA, whose many justifying arguments included that they were "Christianizing" the "pagan" Africans. Frederick Douglass commented: "Between the Christianity of this land and the Christianity of Christ, I recognize the widest possible difference — so wide that to receive the one as good, pure, and holy, is of necessity to reject the other as bad, corrupt, and wicked . . . I therefore hate the corrupt, slave-holding, women-whipping, cradle-plundering, partial and hypocritical Christianity of this land. Indeed, I can see no reason but the most deceitful one for calling the religion of this land Christianity."

Bible Belt

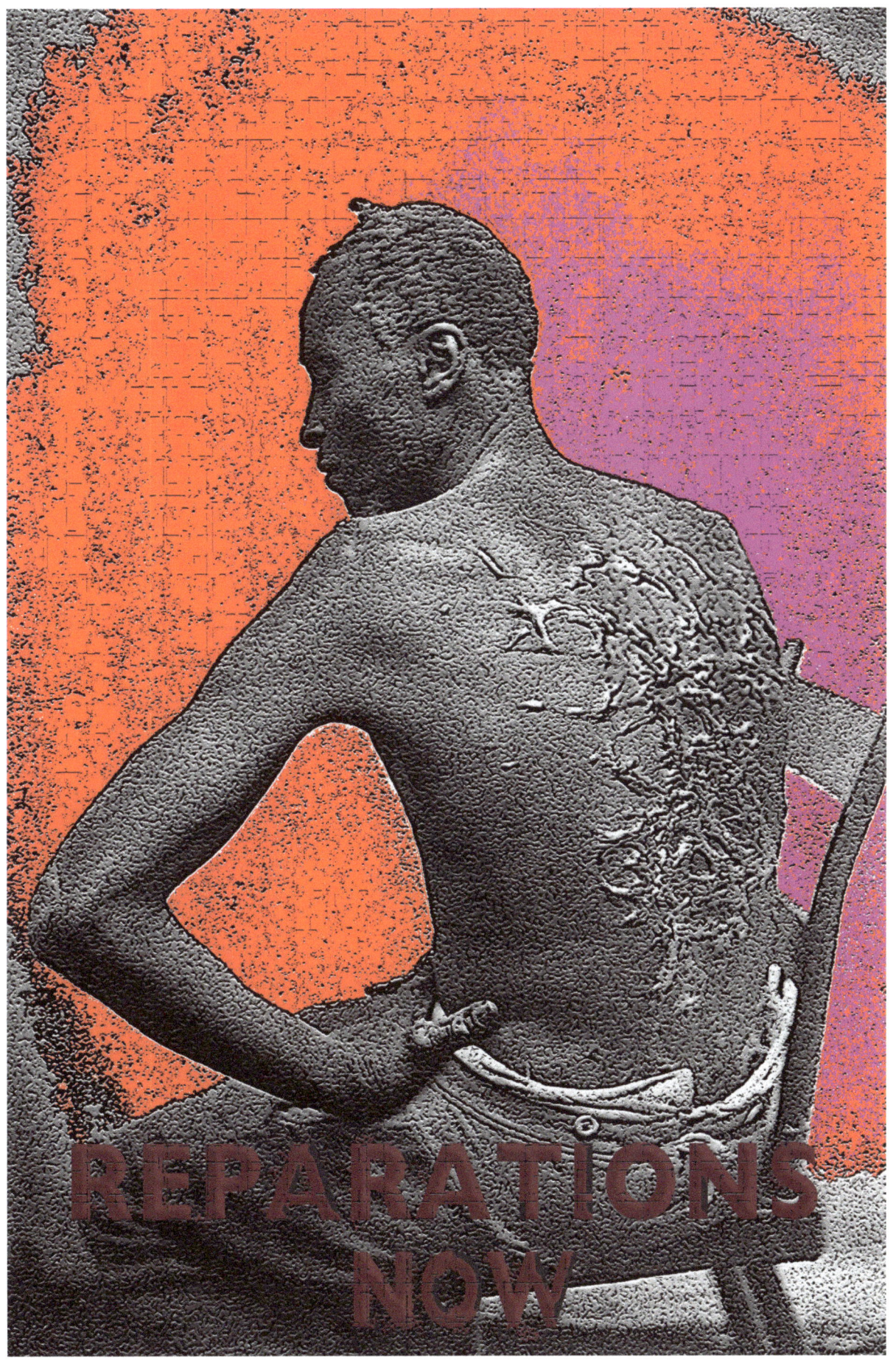

TERUMAH/Offering   Exodus 25 to 27:19

25:31-40 You shall make a lampstand of pure gold, the lampstand shall be made of hammered work; its base and its shaft, its cups, calyxes, and petals shall be of one piece. Six branches shall issue from its sides . . . And on the lampstand itself there shall be four cups shaped like almond blossoms . . . Make its seven lamps . . . and its tongs and fire pans of pure gold. . . . Note well, and follow the patterns for them that are being shown you on the mountain.

In this Torah portion, "God" outdoes Robert Moses as a grand builder and designer, with extensive, precise details about the structure and decoration of the Tabernacle (the *Mishkan*) in which YHVH will dwell as the Israelites sojourn in the wilderness. According to *Midrash Tanhuma*, "the seven lamps of the lampstand" described in this portion "correspond to the seven planets, which pass over the whole earth."

Measurements

By sheer coincidence — ha! — the Sun, which floats about 93 million miles from Earth and measures 109 times wider, and the Moon, which is about 240 thousand miles from Earth and measures only a quarter of its width, look exactly the same size from down here/up here.

If it were different — if, say, our planet were nudged just two percent closer to the Sun's surface temperature of 10 thousand degrees Farenheit — it might not *look* different, but we'd all be dead!

Instead, we sit here in the Goldilocks zone, safe and sound.

Ha!

TETZAVEH/You Shall Command *Exodus 27:20 to 30:10*

28:1-5 You shall bring forward your brother Aaron, with his sons from among the Israelites, to serve Me as priests. . . . Make sacral vestments for your brother Aaron, for dignity and adornment. . . . a breastpiece, an ephod, a robe, a fringed tunic, a headdress, and a sash. . . . make those sacred vestments . . . for priestly service to Me; they, therefore, shall receive the gold, the blue, purple, and crimson yarns, and the fine linen.

"God" turns from infrastructure to fashion design in this Torah portion, detailing every stitch of the outfits that Aaron, brother and comrade to Moses, and his male lineage will wear as priests of Israel. While the people of Israel "were to be 'a kingdom of priests and a holy nation (Exodus 19:6),'" observed Louis Jacobs in *The Jewish Religion*, ". . . there is no doubt that priests in ancient times saw themselves as the aristocrats of the Jewish people." Reza Aslan, in *Zealot*, describes the high priest's "long, sleeveless robe dyed purple (the color of kings) and fringed with dainty tassels and tiny golden bells sewn to the hem; the hefty breastplate, speckled with twelve precious gems, one for each of the tribes of Israel; the immaculate turban sitting . . . like a tiara, fronted by a gold plate on which is engraved the unutterable name of God . . . all of these symbols of ostentation are meant to represent the high priest's exclusive access to God."

Vestments

I've never worn a uniform, not even for sports — and I haven't owned a tie since high school. The last time I wore a suit, in fact, was for a Halloween parade, which I came to as "The Common Cold," with a hankie and a thermometer sticking out of my breast pocket. Most people thought I didn't have a costume on.

Yet for all of my distaste for uniforms, I do remember a period when I was very interested in Mao jackets. I viewed fashion as a form of both class and gender warfare, and figured that if we weren't going to level hierarchy and power relations by being naked all the time, uniformity was the next best thing.

Still, I can't pretend — o, hypocrite! — that at most times in my life I've been indifferent to my own image. I've simply been lucky enough never to work in an office or live in China. The look I prefer is bohemian, cool (literally non-perspiring), hetero, and masculine in a dignified, restrained way. My fashion rules include no visible brand names, and no shorts, boots, baseball caps, or epaulets.

I once asked my brother Russ — who lived for eight years as a monk, wearing itchy robes, before returning to civilian life — why he dresses like a square ("like a refugee from K-Mart," is what I actually said). He thought about it, then replied: "Why would I want to get involved in all that hubba-hubba stuff, 'How do I look, how does she look?'"

Hmm . . . Good question, brother!

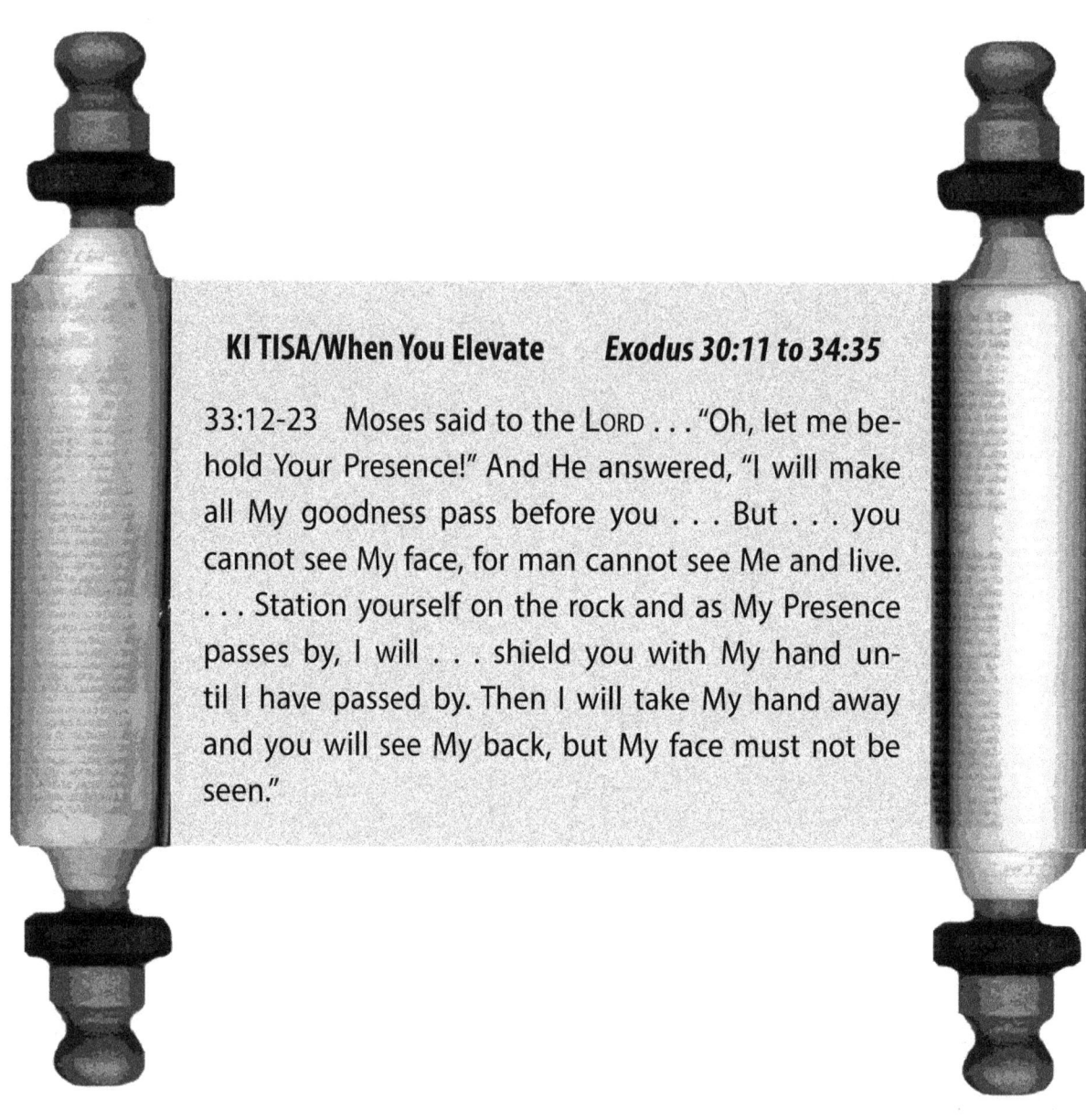

KI TISA/When You Elevate *Exodus 30:11 to 34:35*

33:12-23 Moses said to the Lord . . . "Oh, let me behold Your Presence!" And He answered, "I will make all My goodness pass before you . . . But . . . you cannot see My face, for man cannot see Me and live. . . . Station yourself on the rock and as My Presence passes by, I will . . . shield you with My hand until I have passed by. Then I will take My hand away and you will see My back, but My face must not be seen."

In "Ki Tisa," Moses achieves an unparalleled intimacy with "God" by spending forty days and nights absorbing the Torah atop Mount Sinai. But the Israelites, in his absence, build an idol out of gold, a Golden Calf, and comfort themselves with pagan worship. After convincing "God" not to wipe out his people for their many lapses, Moses begs for an actual view of the divine visage. In Judaism, however, YHVH was always hidden from human view — unlike the Christian God-born-as-man — until the kabbalists came along in the 12th and 13th centuries and, partly in response to Christianity, invented the *sefirot*, emanations of "God" that purportedly grant human beings actual access to the divine.

Emanations

VAYAKHEL/And He Assembled *Exodus 35 to 38:20*

37:1-17 Bezazel made the ark of acacia wood . . . He overlaid it with pure gold, inside and out and he made a gold molding for it round about. He cast four gold rings for it, for its four feet . . . He made poles of acacia wood, overlaid them with gold . . . He made a cover of pure gold . . . He made two cherubim of gold . . . The utensils that were to be upon the table . . . he made of pure gold. . . . He made the lampstand of pure gold.

"It is difficult to fathom the character of this people," Rabbi Abba bar Aba says in the Talmud (*Shekalim* 2b), regarding the Israelites in the wilderness. "When asked to contribute to making the [Golden] Calf, they give; when asked to contribute to building the Tabernacle, they give." Gold is the highest-value gift for the construction of the Tabernacle (offered by "everyone whose heart so moves him," says the Torah portion), and then a master craftsman, Bezazel, uses the precious metal to mark the unique holiness of what is being constructed: YHVH's dwelling place in the wilderness. In making this design choice, both the Israelites and their deity are in thrall to the one element that has probably motivated more greed, and produced more conquest and death, than any other.

Gold

"Abolish the lust for money and Messiah will come."
—*Nachman of Bratslav*
Likutey Moharan

47

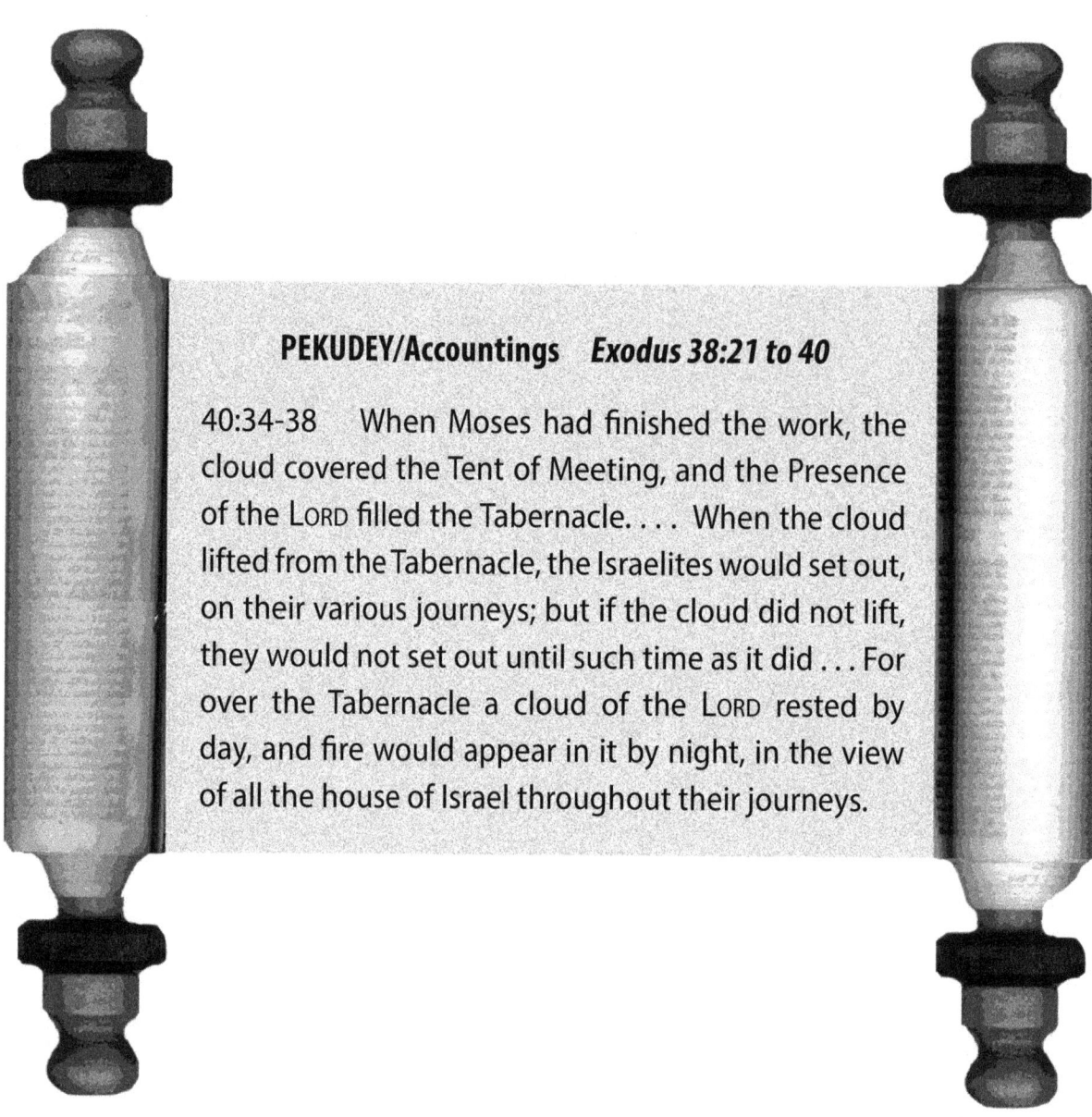

PEKUDEY/Accountings *Exodus 38:21 to 40*

40:34-38 When Moses had finished the work, the cloud covered the Tent of Meeting, and the Presence of the LORD filled the Tabernacle.... When the cloud lifted from the Tabernacle, the Israelites would set out, on their various journeys; but if the cloud did not lift, they would not set out until such time as it did ... For over the Tabernacle a cloud of the LORD rested by day, and fire would appear in it by night, in the view of all the house of Israel throughout their journeys.

Just as the Torah's "God" eventually evolves from a tribal deity to a universal spirit, so has the meaning of the Tabernacle in the wilderness evolved, for many Jews, to encompass the synagogue, the Jewish community, the human heart, and the Earth itself.

LEVITICUS

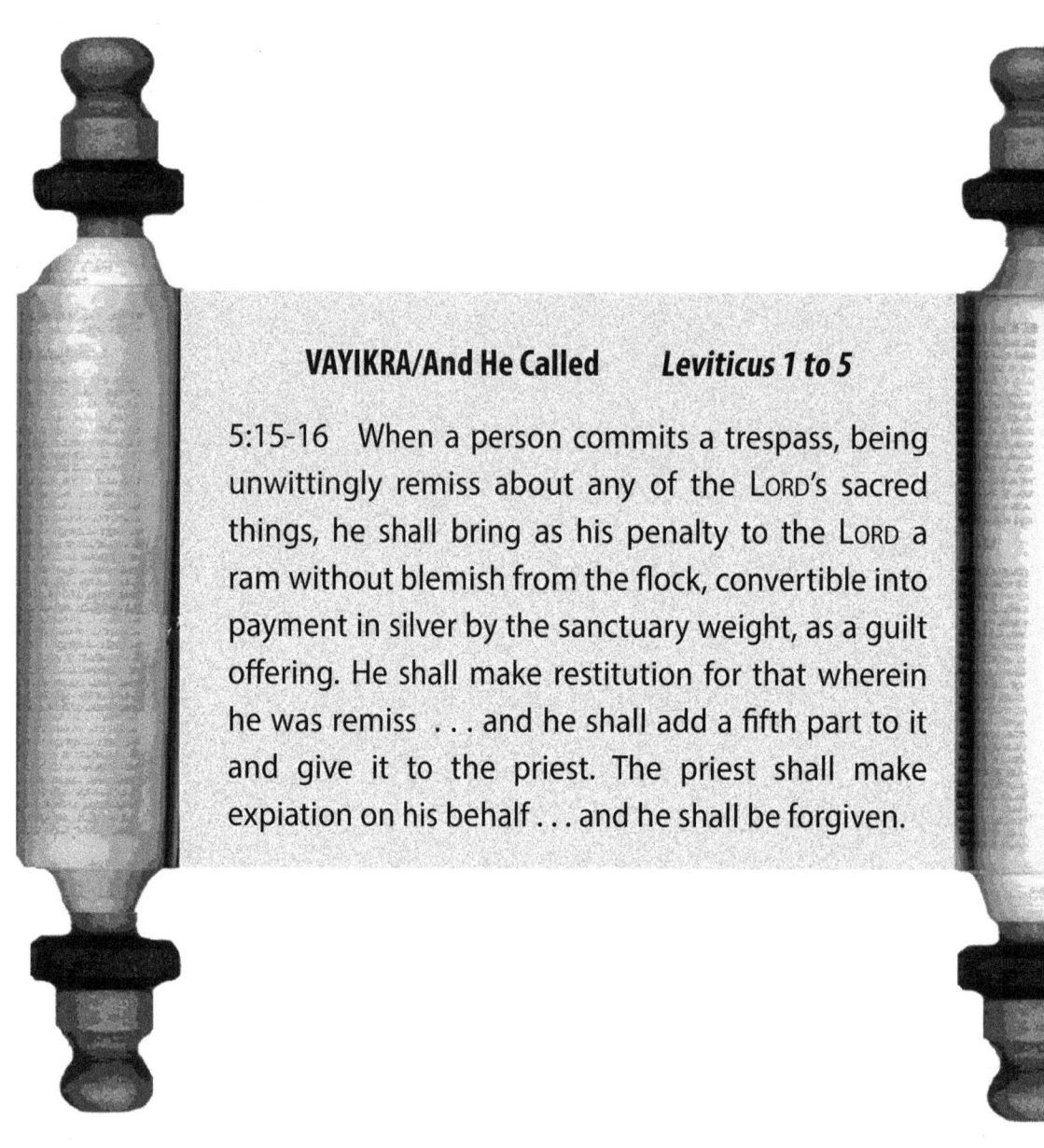

VAYIKRA/And He Called   Leviticus 1 to 5

5:15-16 When a person commits a trespass, being unwittingly remiss about any of the Lord's sacred things, he shall bring as his penalty to the Lord a ram without blemish from the flock, convertible into payment in silver by the sanctuary weight, as a guilt offering. He shall make restitution for that wherein he was remiss . . . and he shall add a fifth part to it and give it to the priest. The priest shall make expiation on his behalf . . . and he shall be forgiven.

The Book of Leviticus begins with careful instructions for the animal and grain sacrifices that are to be made when people sin, intentionally or otherwise. "A person is always responsible," notes the Mishnah (*Baba Kamma* 2.6), "whether their act is intentional or inadvertent, whether they are awake or asleep." Other sacrifices are set forth for people seeking favor from "God." Worship in the Tabernacle — later, in the Jerusalem Temple — involved extensive animal sacrifice and a centralized priesthood. However, once the obliteration of Jerusalem by Rome in the 1st and 2nd centuries led to the dispersal of the Jews and the decentralization of Judaism, the healing of sin was largely prescribed through *teshuvah* (repentance), *tefillah* (prayer), and *tzedakah* (charity).

TZAV/Command! Leviticus 6 to 8

7:37-38 Such are the rituals of the burnt offering, the meal offering, the sin offering, the guilt offering, the offering of ordination, and the sacrifice of well-being, with which the Lord charged Moses on Mount Sinai, when He commanded that the Israelites present their offerings to the Lord, in the wilderness of Sinai.

For ancient nomadic and farming peoples, religious sacrifice, as prescribed in "Tzav," meant surrendering a living animal or crop, and suspending routine activity to make the journey to the place of sacrifice. The danger of such a ritual becoming a rote activity — a system of taxation more than of worship — is noted in several haftorah readings (from the Bible's prophetic books, which are organized in meaningful conjunction with the Torah portions), including the one from the Book of Jeremiah that accompanies "Tzav." Yet the *absence* of sacrifice in modern worship also threatens to render it abstract and self-centered. All of this begs the question: How can a standardized ritual or text serve to awaken rather than deaden us?

The answer that the Talmud repeatedly points to is *tzedakah* — charitable giving in the name of social justice, which the rabbis saw as the greatest tool for awakening the soul.

Charity Saves from Death

Rabbi Eleazar said: Greater is he who does charity than he who offers all the sacrifices. *Sukkah 49b*

It is told of Rabbi Tarfon that although he was very wealthy he did not give many gifts to the poor. Once, Rabbi Akiba met him and said, "Master, would you like me to purchase one or two towns for you?" He replied, "Yes," and handed Akiba 4,000 gold denars. Akiba took the money and gave it all to the poor. Later, Tarfon saw Akiba and asked, "Where are the towns you purchased for me?" Akiba took him by the hand to the study house, and brought over a child holding the book of Psalms, and made Tarfon read and read until he came to the verse, "He has given to the needy; his righteousness lasts forever." Then Akiba said, "This is the town I bought for you." At that, Rabbi Tarfon kissed him and said, "You are my teacher and my guide." And he gave him more money to distribute. *Kallah 2*

Rabbi Joshua taught: More than what the householder does for the poor person, the poor person does for the householder. *Gittin 7b*

SHEMINI/Eighth Day   Leviticus 9 to 11

11: 46-47 These are the instructions concerning animals, birds, all living creatures that move in water, and all creatures that swarm on Earth, for distinguishing between the unclean and the clean, between the living things that may be eaten and the living things that may not be eaten.

Stewardship of Creation is assigned to human beings in the Garden of Eden when "the Holy One," according to *Ecclesiastes Rabbah* 7:13, took Adam "and led him around all the trees of the Garden . . . and said to him: Behold My works how beautiful, how splendid they are. All that I have created, I created for your sake. Take care that you do not become corrupt and thus destroy My world. For once you become corrupt, there is no one after you to repair it." Nevertheless, throughout history, civilizations have interpreted stewardship to mean domination, and have made mincemeat of their environments. Only now, during Earth's Sixth Extinction (to use Elizabeth Kolbert's phrase), are more and more human beings belatedly awakening to what Rabbi Judah HaNasi declared in the Talmud (*Shabbat* 77b): "Of all that the Holy One created, not a single thing is useless."

Macht Fried

TAZRIA/She Bears Seed   Leviticus 12 to 13

12: 2-5   When a woman at childbirth bears a male, she shall be unclean seven days; she shall be unclean as at the time of her menstrual infirmity.... She shall remain in a state of blood purification for thirty-three days: she shall not touch any consecrated thing, nor enter the sanctuary until her period of purification is completed. If she bears a female, she shall be unclean two weeks as during her menstruation...

Rabbi Phyllis Ocean-Berman has generously interpreted the Torah's description of postpartum (and menstrual) "uncleanness" and confinement for women as a way to preserve a new mother's well-being and self-possession at one of the most intense times of her life. "I remember very clearly," she writes *(Philadelphia Jewish Voice)*, "that indeed there is a period of time right after you've given birth that you want and need to be separated from the community. Your community narrows down to the baby right in your arms..." She observes that other experiences that Torah sees as fostering "uncleanness" — for example, encountering a human corpse — are similarly intense and need to be absorbed and gotten over before a person can return to normalcy.

The Baby Boom

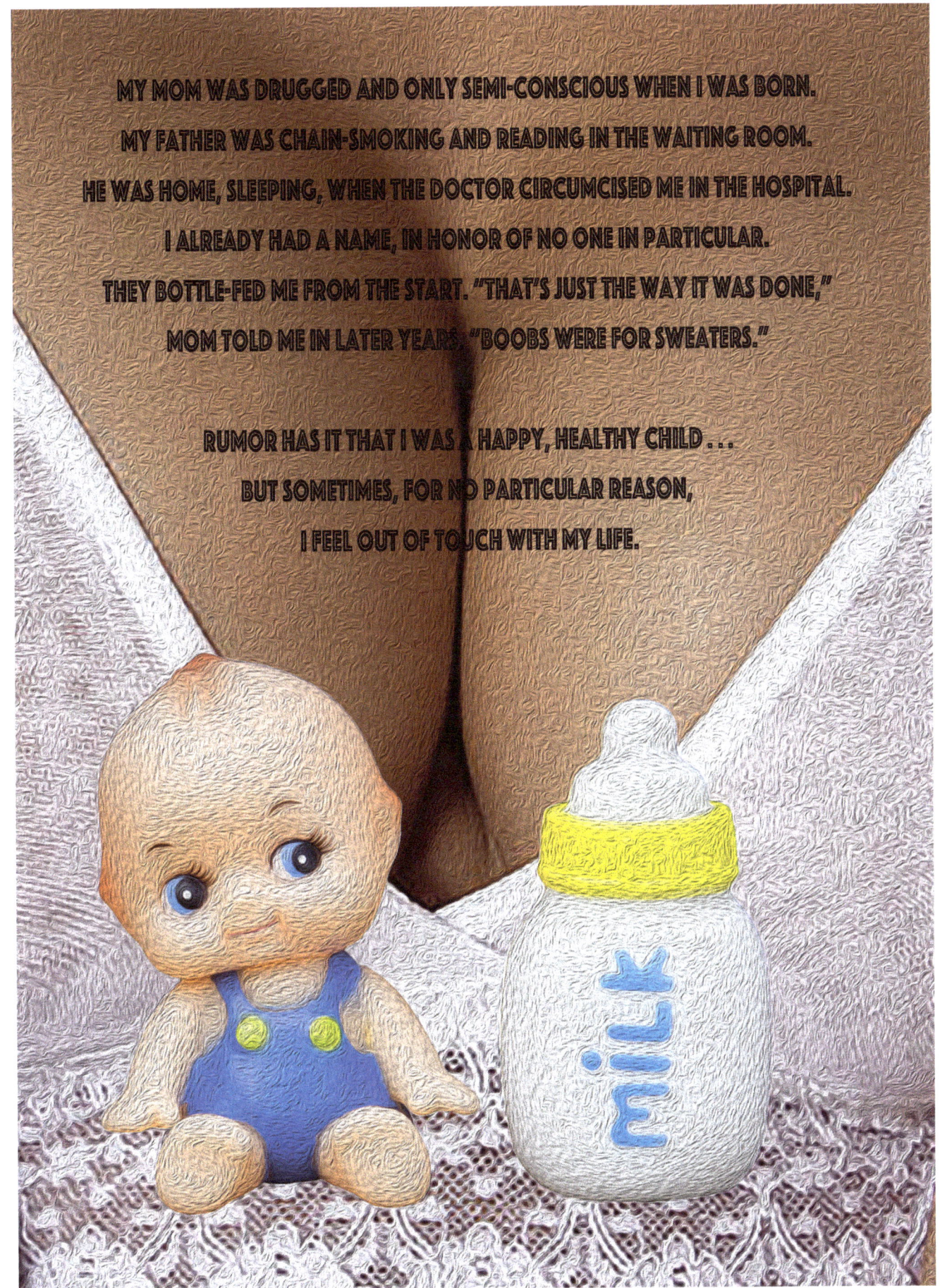

My mom was drugged and only semi-conscious when I was born.
My father was chain-smoking and reading in the waiting room.
He was home, sleeping, when the doctor circumcised me in the hospital.
I already had a name, in honor of no one in particular.
They bottle-fed me from the start. "That's just the way it was done,"
Mom told me in later years, "boobs were for sweaters."

Rumor has it that I was a happy, healthy child...
but sometimes, for no particular reason,
I feel out of touch with my life.

This section of "Metzora" deals with Canaanite houses taken over by the Hebrews that "God," for whatever reason, has afflicted with "an eruptive plague," in which case the owner must go to the priest for a house inspection and ritual of cleansing and expiation. Some Jewish authorities, according to the Reform Movement's *The Torah, a Modern Commentary,* regarded the contamination of houses "as a first warning to sinners."

The Crimson Stuff

Shortly after I was born, in 1951, my parents and several other young Jewish couples moved to St. Albans, Queens, where they were able to buy private houses for very reasonable prices because all the white people in the area were running away from their Black neighbors. My parents' motivation was not at all mercenary, however. They and the others were members of the Communist Party, USA, and they were making the move in order to show that racism did not have to control the New York City housing market. Good for them!

I was too young to have any but the vaguest memories of the house, and I never really asked my parents what it was like to live as white people in an increasingly Black neighborhood. I just know from family lore that my older brother Russ was soon the only white kid in his class; that his best friend was named Gary; and that two older kids with the jazzy names Bobo and Skeeter were among the children who hung out at our house.

When I was four, my parents separated for a year, so they sold the house — the only house they would ever own — and Russ and I moved with our mother to the very unintegrated Queens neighborhood of Forest Hills.

In my earliest clear memory, I'm standing in front of our new garden apartment in Forest Hills, feeling completely bewildered.

AKHAREI MOT/After the Death   *Leviticus 16 to 18*

16: 29-34 And this shall be to you a law for all time: In the seventh month, on the tenth day of the month, you shall practice self-denial . . . For on this day atonement shall be made for you to cleanse you of all your sins; you shall be clean before the Lord. It shall be a sabbath of complete rest for you, and you shall practice self-denial . . . This shall be to you a law for all time: to make atonement for the Israelites for all their sins once a year.

"Once," according to *Avot de Rabbi Natan*, a collection of commentaries collected from the 3rd to 10th centuries, "as Rabbi Yohanan was walking out of Jerusalem, Rabbi Joshua followed him, and, upon seeing the Temple in ruins, he said: 'Woe unto us that this place is in ruins, the place where atonement was made for Israel's iniquities!' Rabbi Yohanan replied: 'My son, do not grieve — we have another means of atonement which is as effective. What is it? It is deeds of loving-kindness . . .'"

Atonement

KEDOSHIM/Holy Ones   Leviticus 19 to 20

19:17-18   You shall not hate your kinsfolk in your heart. Reprove your kinsman but incur no guilt because of him. You shall not take vengeance or bear a grudge against your countrymen. Love your fellow as yourself: I am the Lord.

"Why was the Second Temple destroyed," asks the Talmud (*Yoma* 9b), "seeing that, during the time it stood, people occupied themselves with Torah, observance of precepts, and the practice of charity? Because, during the time it stood, hatred without rightful cause prevailed. This should teach you that hatred without rightful cause is deemed so grave as all the three sins of idolatry, sexual immorality, and bloodshed together."

EMOR/Speak to   *Leviticus 21 to 24*

23:22 And when you reap the harvest of your land, you shall not reap all the way to the edges of your field, or gather the gleanings of your harvest; you shall leave them for the poor and the stranger: I the Lord am your God.

The economic philosophy of the Torah is best expressed in Deuteronomy 8:11, when "God" warns the Israelites: "When you have eaten your fill and have built fine houses to live in . . . beware lest your heart grow haughty and you . . . say to yourselves, 'My own power and the might of my own hand have won this wealth for me.' Remember that it is the Lord your God who gives you the power to get wealth . . ." From this understanding that "God" is the provider flows a sense of responsibility about sharing wealth that is exemplified in "Emor," in which the right of poor people to share in the harvest is established. This right will be exercised by Ruth in the Book of Ruth, leading to her marriage to Boaz — and from their union, joining a non-Jewish woman and a Jewish aristocrat, will come the line of King David and the not-yet-arrived messiah. The Talmud (*Gittin* 61a) further extends the gleaning right to "the poor of the heathen," that is, to non-Jews, "for the sake of peace."

BEHAR/On the Mount   Leviticus 25 to 26:2

25:3-13   Six years you may sow your field and six years you may prune your vineyard and gather in the yield. But in the seventh year the land shall have a sabbath of complete rest, a sabbath of the Lord . . . You shall count off seven weeks of years — seven times seven years . . . and you shall hallow the fiftieth year. You shall proclaim release throughout the land for all its inhabitants. It shall be a jubilee for you: each of you shall return to his holding . . .

Debts are cancelled, Hebrew slaves are freed, and land is returned to its original owners every fiftieth year in the economic system imagined in "Behar." Its declaration of this Jubilee Year is engraved on the Liberty Bell, an iconic symbol of American freedom and independence. The Torah also calls for a "sabbath of the land" every seven years, in which the land is left fallow and the community lives on its accumulated wealth. Overall, the Torah's vision is one of sustainability, modest growth, and economic justice, with both debts and fortunes not allowed to accumulate for more than half a century. If only.

In this final portion of Leviticus, "God" offers blessings of prosperity, fruitfulness, and peace to the Israelites if they are obedient to the Torah's commandments, and a menu of curses — including environmental disaster ("skies like iron . . . earth like copper . . . the land desolate"), insecurity ("a sword against you" and "pestilence among you"), starvation-based cannibalism, and no escape from mortal enemies — if the Israelites disobey the commandments. The portion also reiterates the fundamental economic law of Judaism: that "the Earth is the Lord's," as Psalm 24 puts it, "and all of its fruits" — therefore human beings should perceive their wealth and well-being as blessings, attended by responsibilities, rather than as entitlements or accomplishments.

8½ Planets

If everyone on Earth lived my lifestyle, how many planets would it take to sustain us? That was the nub of a questionnaire at the website of "Marketplace," the NPR business show — which I went online to fill out, figuring we'd need just one planet, or maybe a planet and a moon, if everyone lived like me.

I live rurally, after all, in a 1,200-square-foot house. Much of its energy comes from solar and wood. We work at home, we try to buy local, and we're not really big-time shoppers.

So when I saw my score — 8½ planets! — I was deeply disturbed. Three factors defined my lifestyle as excessive: 1) The wine and coffee we drink comes from far away; 2) We do a *lot* of driving; 3) Susan flies several times each year for work.

Eight-and-a-half planets, just for that! We could give up French wines, of course, but we really had no choice with transportation — there aren't even bike paths around here! To get them, I'd have to become a full-time organizer, just to whittle a few miles off our score. (And organizers do a lot of driving!)

I realized, then, that my solar panels aren't enough. Giving up meat isn't enough. Even a worldwide redistribution of wealth wouldn't be enough, as long as we're all embedded in a make-sell-use-throw-away system.

Yes, there are choices I can make that would ease my conscience — I want to be able to claim innocence just as much as anyone! — but the reality is that my modest life demands multiple planets, and I'm not yet ready to become a renunciate monk.

Signing off from the "Marketplace" website, I brewed myself a cup of coffee (make that nine planets), then I picked up my guitar (probably made of endangered wood) and resumed learning how to play the Gershwins' great number, "They Can't Take That Away from Me."

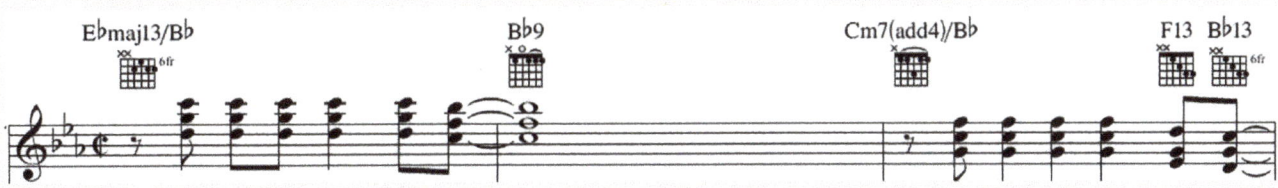

NUMBERS

B'MIDBAR/In the Wilderness   Numbers 1 to 4:20

1:1-3 On the first day of the second month, in the second year following the exodus from the land of Egypt, the Lord spoke to Moses in the wilderness of Sinai, in the Tent of Meeting, saying: Take a census of the whole Israelite community by the clans of its ancestral houses, listing the names, every male, head by head. You and Aaron shall record them by their groups, from the age of twenty years up, all those in Israel who are able to bear arms.

The Book of Numbers begins with a census oriented towards the building of a military force for the purpose of conquering Canaan, the "Promised Land." The men "able to bear arms" number over 600,000. (They're going to need a lot of manna!) In Jewish law, noted Conservative Judaism's Rabbi Ismar Schorsch, the procedure of counting heads always "aroused anxiety and was never enacted lightly," in recognition that "the taking of a census was generally associated with conscription for war . . ."

The Lottery

I never would have gone to fight in that war. It was useless, endless, and filled with murderous atrocities. It had nothing to do with the security of the America I loved. It was a criminal war, the product of sick men.

I would've fled to Canada, unashamedly. Or pretended to be gay. Or taken speed for ten days and pretended to be out of my mind. I knew guys who had done each of these successfully, and only one who had actually fought in the war. Well, no matter: I had a 2-S student deferment.

Then they abolished student deferments and instituted a Selective Service Lottery. For my birth year 1951, the lottery was held on July 1, 1970. My distinct memory is that I drew a number in the low 300s, but Google says that the number for my birthday, December 18th, was #208, in a year when the the cut-off number for the draft was 125. That's a slightly closer shave than I recall. Makes me wonder if, somehow, my birthdate wasn't mistakenly entered as December 17th: #315.

Either way, I'm a lucky son of a ~~gun~~ gumball!

NASO/Elevate! *Numbers 4:21 to 7*

6:22-27 The L ORD spoke to Moses: Speak to Aaron and his sons. Thus shall you bless the people of Israel. Say to them:
The L ORD bless you and protect you!
The L ORD deal kindly and graciously with you!
The L ORD bestow His favor upon you and grant you peace.

The "Priestly Blessing" recited in "Naso" is accompanied by a two-handed gesture, with each hand approximating the Hebrew letter *shin*, for "Shaddai." This is a name for "God" that appears four dozen times in the Torah and has nearly as many translations. Some of the Talmudic rabbis and Jewish mystics interpreted it to mean, "The One Who Said [during the process of Creation]: 'Enough.'" Other translations include "Destroyer" and "Breasted God(dess)." Because of the gesture, the blessing is known in the rabbinic literature as "raising of the hands."

Raising of the Hands

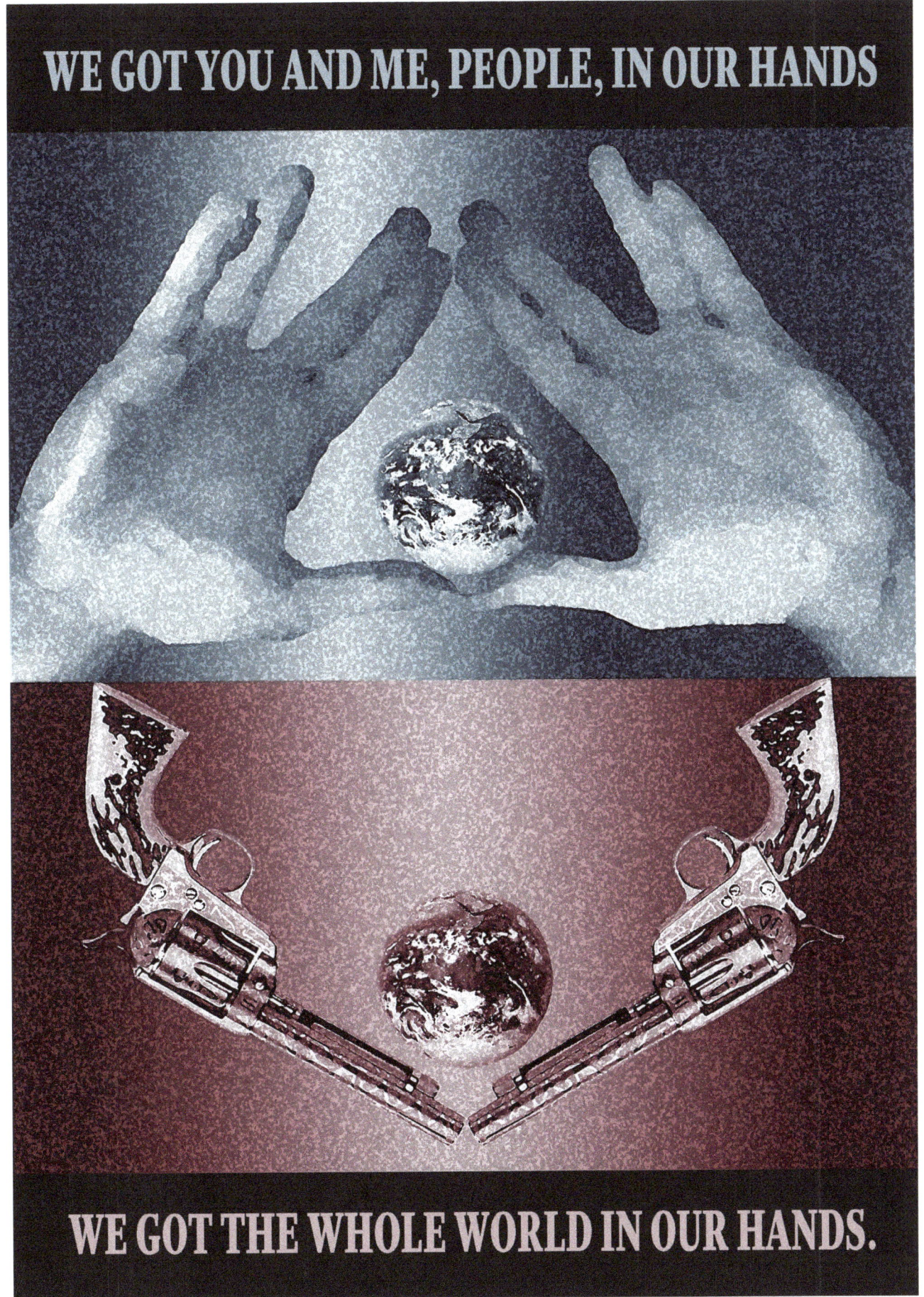

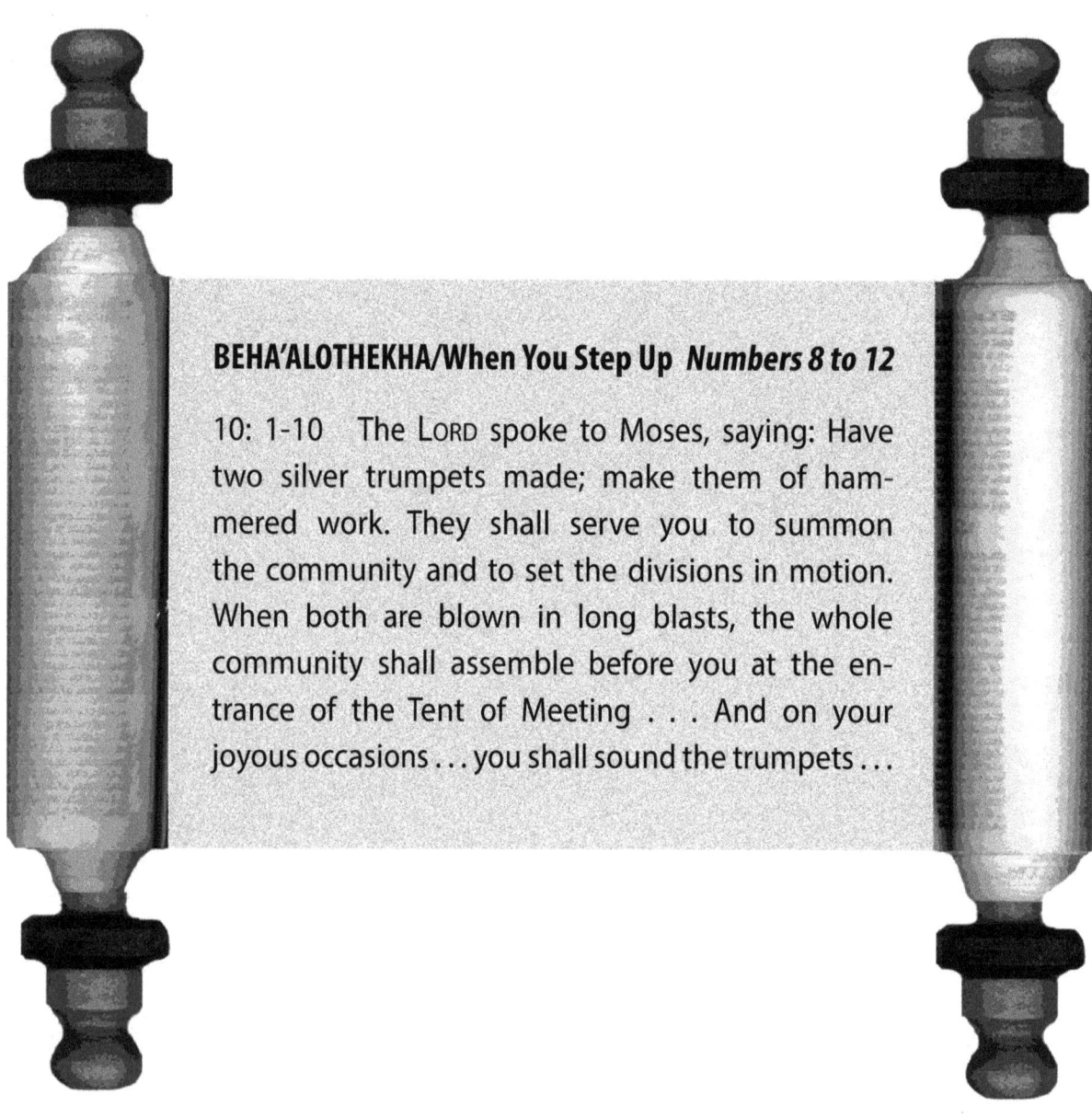

BEHA'ALOTHEKHA/When You Step Up *Numbers 8 to 12*

10: 1-10   The Lord spoke to Moses, saying: Have two silver trumpets made; make them of hammered work. They shall serve you to summon the community and to set the divisions in motion. When both are blown in long blasts, the whole community shall assemble before you at the entrance of the Tent of Meeting . . . And on your joyous occasions . . . you shall sound the trumpets . . .

The trumpets that "God" orders made in this Torah portion are to be blown to mobilize the people both for war and for the celebration of festivals. The Talmud includes some descriptions of ecstatic goings-on during Sukkot, the harvest festival, when the Levites — the tribe that serves the Temple and its priests — stood on "the fifteen steps leading down from the Court of the Israelites to the Court of the Women" and "played their music," while "two priests stood by the upper gate . . . each with a trumpet in hand."

"He who has not seen the rejoicing at the place of the water-drawing," the Mishnah declares (*Sukkah* 5:1), "has never in his life seen true rejoicing."

Silver Trumpets

They called him "Pops" because he was the father of our country.

He transformed jazz into a music of complex improvisational soloing. "He is the beginning and the end of music in America," said his friend, Bing Crosby.

For most of his life, Pops wore a Star of David around his neck to honor the Karnofskys, a ragpicking and coal-hauling family in New Orleans, who took him in as a small boy, paid and fed him, and helped him buy his first cornet. "I had a long admiration for the Jewish people," he later wrote. "Especially for their long time of courage, taking so much abuse for so long."

"[T]he genius of this nation at its best," said Harold Bloom, "is indeed Walt Whitman and Louis Armstrong."

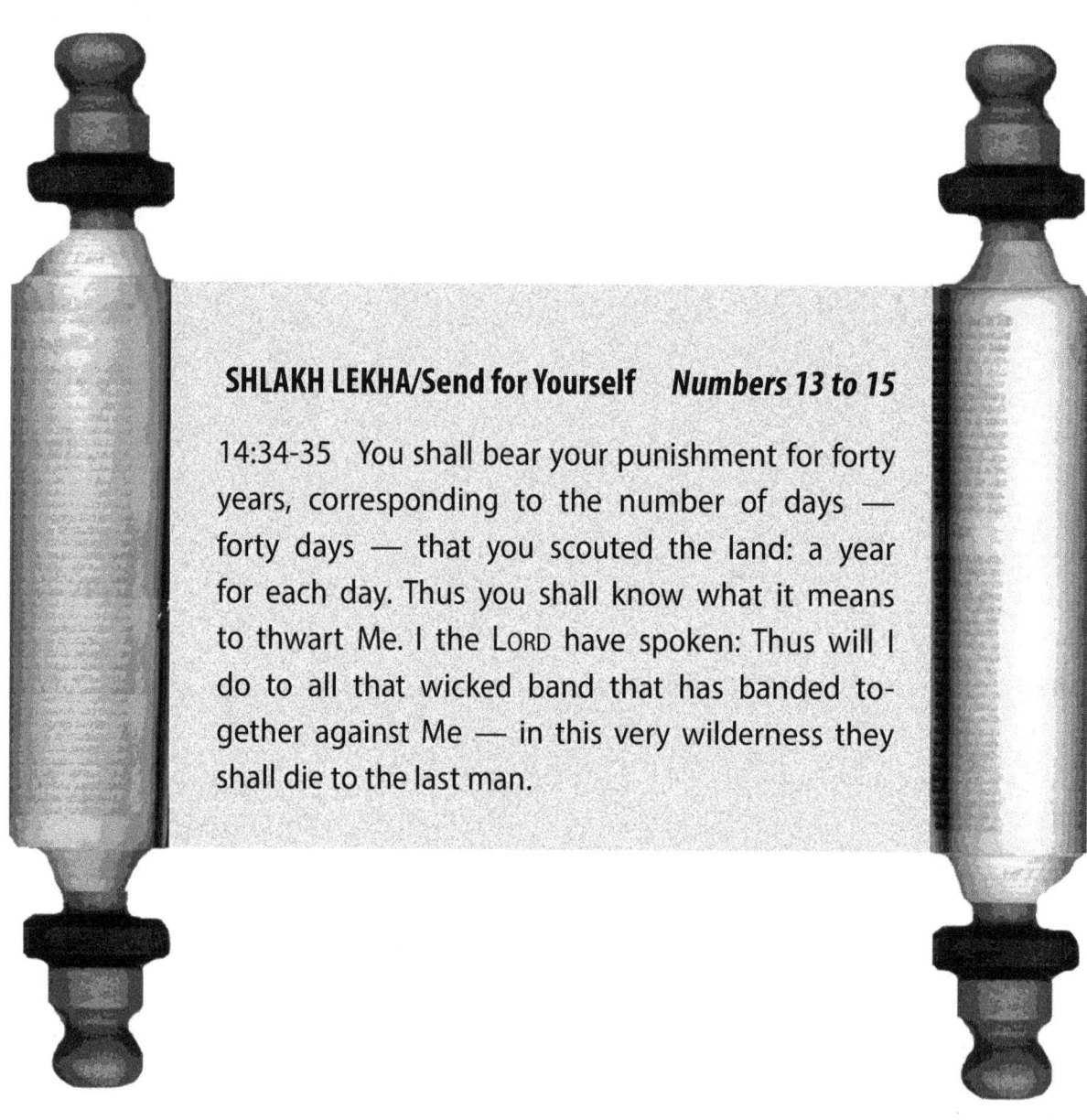

SHLAKH LEKHA/Send for Yourself   *Numbers 13 to 15*

14:34-35   You shall bear your punishment for forty years, corresponding to the number of days — forty days — that you scouted the land: a year for each day. Thus you shall know what it means to thwart Me. I the Lord have spoken: Thus will I do to all that wicked band that has banded together against Me — in this very wilderness they shall die to the last man.

When Moses, at YHWH's command, sends scouts into Canaan, they return with false scary reports of "men of great size" and "cities [that] are fortified and very large." These intimidating rumors set the Israelites to shouting at Moses and Aaron: "Why is the Lord taking us to that land to fall by the sword? . . . better for us to go back to Egypt!" Outraged by their disloyalty, "God" punishes them with a curse: Their entire generation will linger in the wilderness for forty years and die without entering the Promised Land. In the end, even Moses will not be permitted to enter.

Numbers

In my early thirties I lived at 41 Wyckoff Street. I worked at 41 Union Square West. My phone number ended in 4110. My eye doctor was at 41 W 14 Street. I wondered if something dramatic was going to happen in my 41st year. A prime number. Just one past the Biblical 40. Maybe I would die. Or maybe my ship would come in. I waited. Had kids. Bought a house. Turned 41. Nothing unusual happened.

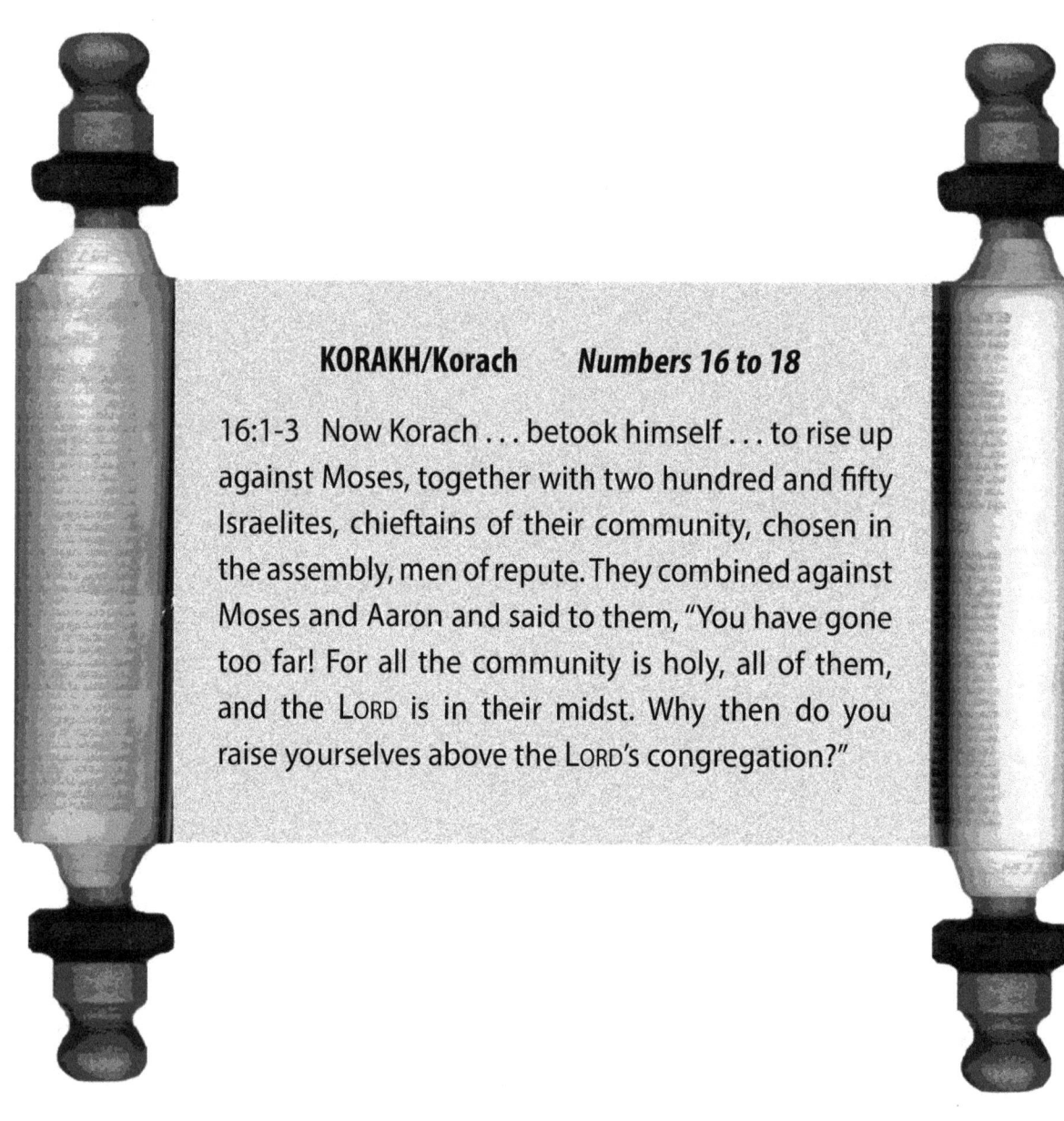

KORAKH/Korach   Numbers 16 to 18

16:1-3 Now Korach . . . betook himself . . . to rise up against Moses, together with two hundred and fifty Israelites, chieftains of their community, chosen in the assembly, men of repute. They combined against Moses and Aaron and said to them, "You have gone too far! For all the community is holy, all of them, and the Lord is in their midst. Why then do you raise yourselves above the Lord's congregation?"

In this Torah portion, a sizeable contingent of rebels, under the leadership of Korach, a cousin to Moses and Aaron, argues against the brothers' authority. The rebels are then murdered by "God" in a grim demonstration: "[T]he ground under them burst asunder, and the Earth opened its mouth and swallowed them up . . ." This story of revolution versus revelation, in which "God" clearly prefers the "divine right of kings" to the demands of a revolutionary committee, makes "Korach" one of the Torah's more challenging political scenarios. While the Talmud overrides any ambiguity in the story by portraying Korach as a self-serving demagogue, it also gives voice to his accusation that the laws and sacrifices that Moses has promulgated are imposing genuine hardship upon the people. The Book of Numbers will also report (26:12) that "the sons of Korach did not die," perhaps implying that, in the words of Thomas Jefferson, "a little rebellion now and then is a good thing."

KHUKAT/Law   Numbers 19 to 22:1

20:23-29   At Mount Hor, on the boundary of the land of Edom, the L<small>ORD</small> said to Moses and Aaron, "Let Aaron be gathered to his kin"... Moses stripped Aaron of his vestments and put them on his son Eleazar, and Aaron died there on the summit of the mountain. When Moses and Eleazar came down from the mountain, the whole community knew that Aaron had breathed his last. All the house of Israel bewailed Aaron thirty days.

While it is Moses' sister Miriam who bravely saves him in his infancy, it is his brother Aaron who enables him to take on the mantle of liberator. Aaron serves as spokesperson for Moses, (who describes himself as "slow of speech") and joins him in daring to confront Pharaoh. While Moses will be known to his people as a stern lawgiver, Aaron will have a reputation as a populist and mediator.

"From the beginning of the world's creation until the present," observes the Midrash *(Tanhuma Shemot)*, "you find brothers who hate each other — Cain hated Abel and slew him, Ishmael hated Isaac and sought to slay him, Esau hated Jacob, and the tribe fathers hated Joseph." But of Moses and Aaron "it is said, 'Behold, how good and how pleasant it is for brethren to dwell together in unity'" (Psalm 133).

Brothers

Sometimes, I'm sure, he wanted to kill me. I was a very pushy younger brother. But when he wasn't teasing me, he taught me about everything cool: Chicago blues, late-night radio, street games, Sherlock Holmes, Martha and the Vandellas, All-Star Baseball, mandalas, Jimi Hendrix, and much, much more.

We've been adults, now, for over half a century, but somehow I'm still his pesky kid brother.

BALAK/Balak   Numbers 22:2 to 25:9

25:1-9   While Israel was staying at Shittim, the people profaned themselves by whoring with the Moabite women, who invited the people to the sacrifices for their god . . . . Thus Israel attached itself to Baal-peor, and the Lord was incensed. . . The Lord said to Moses, "Take all the ringleaders and have them publicly impaled . . ."

The Israelites have marched onto "the steppes of Moab, across the Jordan from Jericho," and are instilling dread in the Moabites. One way the Moabite men deal with the threat is by trying to seduce the invaders with their women and their ways, including their religion, which worships the god of their mountain, Peor. The ever-jealous YHVH punishes the Israelites harshly with executions and a consuming plague that kills 24,000.

Another Song of Ascent

See that woman at the front of the line,
Legs so polished you can see them shine . . .
Warning! Stay back 100 feet.

    Look at the waitress in her cocktail dress.
    She's your server, don't you make a mess.
    Warning! Stay back 100 feet.

        There's so much beauty of the womanly kind,
        Making so much effort but don't pay no mind.
        You're just a fool if you look and look,
        And if you keep looking it'll be mistook.

            See those nubiles with their giggling style.
            They're out half-naked but don't be beguiled.
            Warning! Stay back 100 feet.

                And look at that exec in her pencil skirt.
                You want to catch up with her, you want to flirt.
                Warning! Stay back 100 feet.

                    There's beauty here, beauty there.
                    Gorgeous women everywhere.
                    But you're just a fool if you look and look,
                    And if you keep looking it'll be mistook.

                So step back, fellas — being civilized
                Means keeping your libido
                    an appropriate size.
                Warning! Stay back 100 feet.

PINKHAS/Phineas   Numbers 25:10 to 30:1

27:1-6 The daughters of Zelophehad . . . came forward. . . . They stood before Moses . . . and the whole assembly . . . and they said, "Our father died in the wilderness . . . and he has left no sons. Let not our father's name be lost to his clan just because he had no son! Give us a holding among our father's kinsmen!" . . . And the Lord said to Moses "The plea of Zelophehad's daughters is just . . ."

The daughters of Zelophehad, says the Midrash *(Sifre Numbers)*, "decided that the mercies of flesh and blood are not like the mercies of Him who is everywhere. Flesh and blood is apt to be more merciful to males than to females. But He who spoke and brought the world into being is different — His mercies are for males as well as females, His mercies being for all."

Shulamith

I met Shulamith in the lobby of the American Jewish Congress on the Upper East Side of Manhattan, in 1978. We were both applicants for the AJC CETA Project, a government program that paid artists a living wage to serve community organizations as artists-in-residence while also having ample studio time.

I had just signed on as part-time assistant editor of *Jewish Currents*, a magazine that would eventually become the central address of my work life. One of its board members, active in the AJC, had urged me to apply for CETA. I was also writing my novel, *BESSIE* — the only one of four I wrote that was published.

Shulamith's book, *The Dialectic of Sex*, published eight years earlier, had already been translated into a dozen languages. She had also co-founded New York Redstockings, a collective of tough, creative feminists, and had edited *Voices of the Women's Liberation Movement*, the first feminist newsletter in the U.S.

I was working at being a feminist, but I knew nothing about Redstockings or *The Dialectic of Sex*. Still, after talking with her for maybe twenty minutes, I thought, *This woman sure deserves this a lot more than I do*. I told her so, then left without an interview.

Shulamith Firestone joined some CETA artists earning $10,000 per year, with health insurance, in New York City.

People are still talking about her influence.

(I've never regretted withdrawing from the competition. Sometimes you've just got to give way.)

MATOT/Tribes Numbers 30:2 to 32

31:3-10 Moses spoke to the people, saying, "Let men be picked out from among you for a campaign, and let them fall upon Midian to wreak the Lord's vengeance on Midian."... They took the field against Midian, as the Lord had commanded Moses, and slew every male.... The Israelites took the women and children of the Midianites captive, and seized as booty all their beasts, all their herds, and all their wealth. And they destroyed by fire all the towns ...

The tribes of Israel have begun their terrible wars of conquest against the peoples of Canaan, whom "God" demands be exterminated, not merely conquered. The Talmud portrays the alleged descendants of these conquered peoples — Africans, Egyptians, Ishmaelites, and Ketureans — petitioning Alexander the Great for the return of their land, only to be conquered once more in debate with Gebiha ben Pesisa, a doorkeeper in the Jerusalem Temple, who craftily cites Torah passages that support the Israelites' right to conquer Canaan. History, as Stefan Zweig wrote in 1936, "keeps her eyes fixed on the victorious, and leaves the vanquished in the shadows."

Pogrom

"The rioting began with the looting of the Jewish shops and the demolition of houses. The mob, finding the military not employed against them and the police witnessing the attacks sympathetically . . . passed from murder and massacre to the violation of Jewish women and girls . . ."

"One Mottel Greenspoon, a glazier, was stunned by a blow from a bludgeon, and the [attackers] mutilated him while still alive. They then choked a child, two years old, and cut out its tongue, while alive . . . The mob then found its way to the loft where the women were concealed, and remained several hours. . . . Thirteen girls and women of ages ranging from 17 to 48 . . . were assaulted by from two to 20 men, and in many cases left for dead . . ."

"All house-breaking and robbery were suspended in the nighttime during the outbreak, and the younger men of the 30 or 40 gangs of rioters went in search of the hidden girls and married women . . . The latest list . . . gives these figures: killed, 44; badly wounded, 83; injured, 500. Houses wrecked, 700; shops and small stores looted and damaged, 600 . . . 10,000 people require relief."

Text: M. Davitt, Within the Pale, The True Story of Anti-Semitic Persecutions in Russia, 1903

MASEI/Journeys   Numbers 33-36

35:30-33 If anyone kills a person, the manslayer may be executed only on the evidence of witnesses; the testimony of a single witness against a person shall not suffice ... You may not accept a ransom for the life of a murderer who is guilty of a capital crime; he must be put to death. ... You shall not pollute the land in which you live; for blood pollutes the land, and the land can have no expiation for blood that is shed on it, except by the blood of him who shed it.

The final Torah portion of the Book of Numbers advocates capital punishment for murder but insists that there be more than one witness in death-penalty cases. "Masei" also establishes "six cities of refuge" in Canaan and beyond "so that anyone who kills a person unintentionally can flee there" and avoid facing blood vengeance, the exacting of revenge by the family of the dead. The killer, however, must remain in the city of refuge to which he flees until the High Priest who is serving at the time dies. Given that young men are disproportionately the ones who commit heedless crimes, including manslaughter, while high priests were likely to be mature men, this law amounts to a young man's quarantine from his home community at least for the span of his dangerous youth.

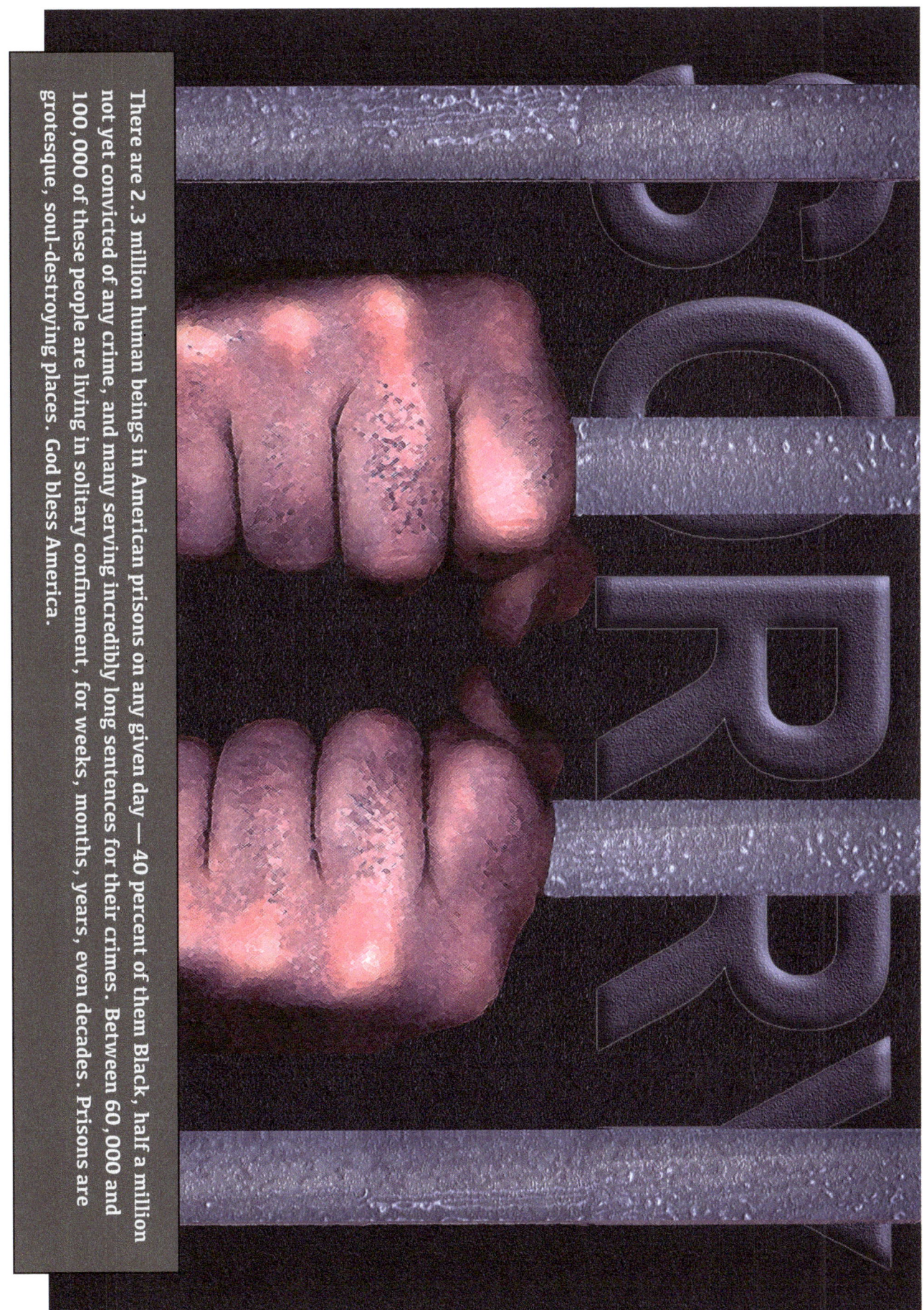

There are 2.3 million human beings in American prisons on any given day — 40 percent of them Black, half a million not yet convicted of any crime, and many serving incredibly long sentences for their crimes. Between 60,000 and 100,000 of these people are living in solitary confinement, for weeks, months, years, even decades. Prisons are grotesque, soul-destroying places. God bless America.

DEUTERONOMY

DEVARIM/Words   Deuteronomy 1 to 3:22

1:35-39 Not one of these men, this evil generation, shall see the good land that I swore to give to your fathers . . . your little ones who you said would be carried off, your children who do not yet know good from bad, they shall enter it; to them will I give it and they shall possess it.

Moses opens the Book of Deuteronomy with a recitation of the wanderings and military campaigns of his people, and an evaluation of their obedience to the will of "God." Because of their hesitancy and prevarication about entering the land they are to conquer, their arrival will be delayed by "God" for forty years, time enough for them all to die. Even Moses and Aaron will be denied entry because of their own minor lapse in the wilderness of Zin, where they provided water from a rock but "did not trust Me enough to affirm My sanctity in the sight of the Israelite people," as YHVH complains in Numbers 20:12 — that is, they did not give "God" credit for the miracle. As a result, only those who are young enough not to have experienced slavery in Egypt will enter the Promised Land. Deprived of historical memory, bequeathed a story rather than a lived experience, how and why will they feel called to Jewish identity?

TOYS FOR TATELES & MAMELES

Slinky-Shminky
BE CAREFUL ON THE STAIRCASE WITH THAT THING!

MARGRET & H.A. REY'S Curious George Goes to Shul
Why does the man in the yellow hat always wear a hat?

ROCK'EM - SOCK'EM RABBIS — WORLD'S ONLY FIGHTING RABBIS — "We'll give you such a POTSH!" by Marx

SPEAK YIDDISH, AMELIA BEDELIA!

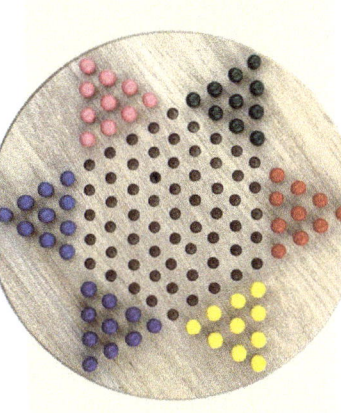

PROMISED LAND TOYS AND GIFTS
"We stand behind our products — way behind!"

Everybody Loves... **Mr. Gefilte Head**

THE HARDY BOYCHIKS — THE TWO-STATE SOLUTION — FRANKLIN W. DIXON

JEWISH IDENTITY in a BOX or a BOOK!

THE LITTLE ENGINE THAT SHOULD by WATTY PIPEK — PLATT & MUNK CLASSICS

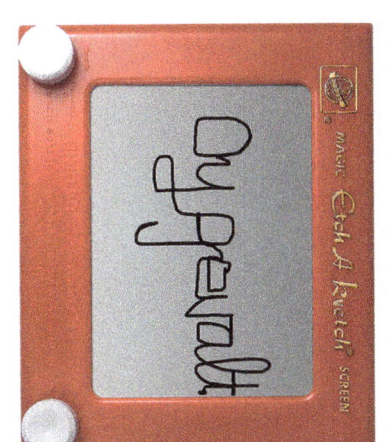

magic Etch A Sketch screen — *Oy gevalt*

VA'ETKHANAN/Pleaded   *Deuteronomy 3:23 to 7:11*

4:10-13   "Gather the people to Me that I may let them hear My words, in order that they may learn to revere Me as long as they live on Earth, and may so teach their children." You came forward and stood at the foot of the mountain. The mountain was ablaze with flames to the very skies, dark with densest clouds. The Lord spoke to you out of the fire . . . He declared to you the covenant . . . the Ten Commandments . . .

Moses continues his recitation of the Hebrew people's experience by reminding them of the revelation at Mount Sinai and again reciting the Ten Commandments. He also importunes the people to "love the Lord your God with all your heart and with all your soul and with all your might," and charges them to "Take to heart these instructions with which I charge you this day" and to "Impress them upon your children."

Impress Them upon Your Children

Do not pollute the Earth.
Do not be cruel to people or animals,
    nor offend their dignity.
Do not believe that what you have
    is what you deserve.
Do not judge people by their looks.
Do not be anxious or hopeless;
    have faith that life is good.
Cultivate pleasure; get outdoors.
Do not allow your passions to rule you
    or to rule others.
Meditate on the interconnection of all
    living things.
Do not take life.
Keep on trucking.

EIKEV/As a Result   *Deuteronomy 7:12 to 11:25*

10:16-19 Cut away, therefore, the thickening about your hearts and stiffen your necks no more. For the Lord our God is God supreme and Lord supreme, the great, the mighty, and the awesome God, who shows no favor and takes no bribe, but upholds the cause of the fatherless and the widow, and befriends the stranger, providing him with food and clothing. — You too must befriend the stranger, for you were strangers in the land of Egypt.

In the previous Torah portion, "Va'Etkhanan," "God" orders the Israelite people to conquer "many nations before you" and "doom them to destruction: grant them no terms and give them no quarter." In "Eikev," He then warns the Israelites not to become arrogant when they take over the Promised Land — not to believe that each one's "own power and the might of my own hand have won this wealth for me" — and not to become indifferent to the suffering of others. This combination of exterminatory ruthlessness and *noblesse oblige* is a Biblical foreshadowing of American history.

Statuary

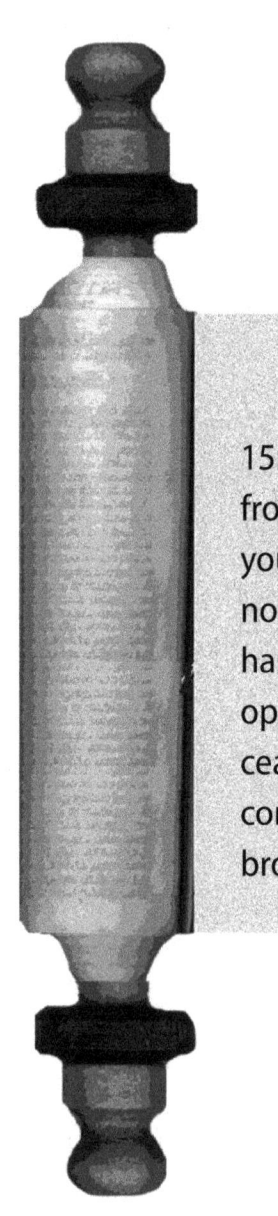

RE'EH/See! *Deuteronomy 11:26 to 16:17*

15:7-11 If there be among you a needy person, from one of your brethren in one of your cities, in your land the Lord your God is giving you, you shall not harden your heart, and you shall not close your hand from your needy brother. Rather, you shall open your hand to him . . . For there will never cease to be needy within the land. Therefore, I command you, you shall open your hand to your brother, to your poor one . . .

"Care of the poor," said Baruch Spinoza, "is incumbent on society as a whole." Spinoza may have been an excommunicant from the Jewish community of his day, but his insight nevertheless reflects the philosophy of the Torah, the Talmud, and the Jewish tradition as a whole. "Shutting one's eye from charity is like worshipping idols," observes the Jerusalem Talmud (*Peah* 4:20). Such idols, in modern terms, might include the Almighty Dollar and the pervasive illusion that wealth is almost entirely the product of a person's virtues and a central determinant of his or her worth as a human being.

The Open Hand

SHOFTIM/Judges   *Deuteronomy 16:18 to 21:9*

17:14-18   If, after you have entered the land that the Lord your God has assigned to you . . . you decide, "I will set a king over me, as do all the nations about me," you shall be free to set a king over yourself, one chosen by the Lord your God. . . . [H]e shall not have many wives, lest his heart go astray; nor shall he amass silver and gold to excess. . . . When he is seated on his royal throne, he shall have a copy of this Teaching written for him on a scroll . . .

The royal throne, says Rabbi Huna in the Midrash *(Esther Rabbah)* "had six steps leading to the seat, which were to remind the king, as he ascended, of the six commandments for rulers: not to multiply horses, wives and gold," as this Torah portion commands, "and not to wrest judgment, show partiality, or accept bribes. Above the throne was a sign: Know before Whom you sit!"

Notwithstanding these standards of kingship, "Shoftim" does grant permission to a people who have escaped oppression by a king — the pharaoh of Egypt — to return themselves to a system of monarchy. This system will produce, as recounted in later books of the Bible, the disappearance of ten of the dozen tribes of Israel, and numerous other tragedies.

IMAGIO

What's with our need to turn people into kings, queens, idols and demigods?

The security of hierarchy? The fantasy of heroism? The intensity of staring at a face that does not stare back?

KI TETZE/When You Go Out   Deuteronomy 21:10 to 25

22:8   When you build a new house, you shall make a parapet for your roof, so that you do not bring bloodguilt on your house if anyone should fall from it.

This passage was extrapolated by the Talmudic rabbis into a category of rules called *s'yag l'torah*, "placing a fence around the Torah," that is, conducting oneself extra carefully so as not to violate any of the Torah's commandments, even accidentally. An example of this is the dietary practice of separating the consumption of meat from the consumption of dairy products by several hours, to ensure that the Torah's commandment, "You shall not boil a young goat in its mother's milk" (Exodus 23:19) is scrupulously obeyed. In general, the principle of "placing a fence around the Torah" has been applied only to personal and communal religious conduct. What about its social implications for the larger world, especially for the kind of scientific and industrial investigations that tamper with the fundamentals of Creation — the atom, the double helix, the climate of the Earth?

For Heaven's Sake

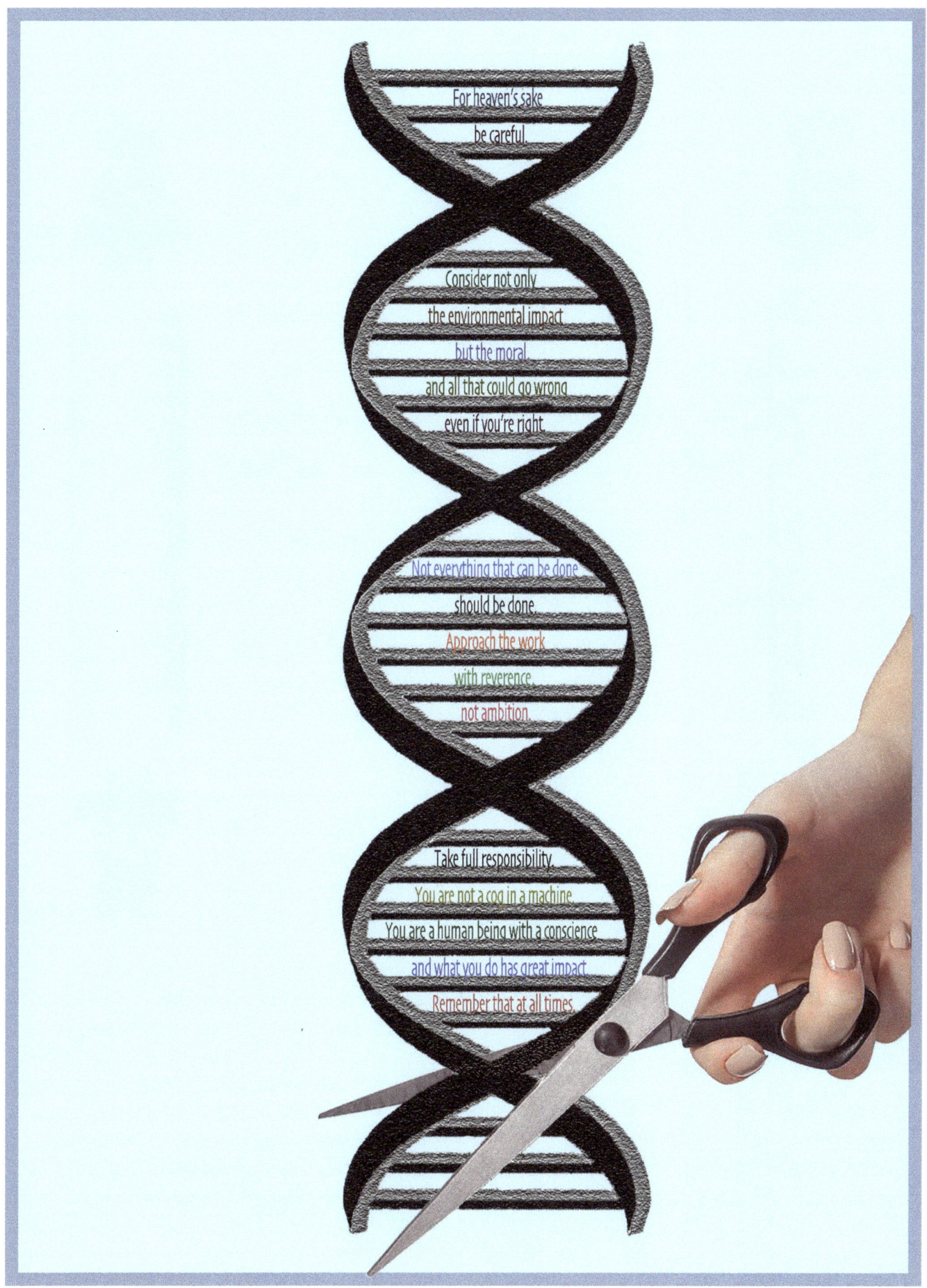

KI TAVO/When You Enter *Deuteronomy 26 to 29:8*

27:2-8 As soon as you have crossed the Jordan into the land that the Lord your God is giving you, you shall set up large stones. . . . And on those stones you shall inscribe every word of this Teaching most distinctly.

"Ki Tavo" enumerates the blessings that will befall the Israelites if they faithfully follow the commandments of "God," and the grotesque curses that will befall them if they are disobedient and heedless.

The covenant between "God" and the Israelites that the Torah describes includes the observance of Rosh Hashanah, Yom Kippur, Passover, and Sukkot. Other Jewish holidays have emerged from history and tradition to create a year-round Jewish calendar that can help attune the mind to a covenantal consciousness of interconnectedness and responsibility.

Give Attention

Give attention to your community
Give attention to yourself
Give attention to sky
Give attention to rain
Give attention to learning
Give attention to darkness
Give attention to trees
Give attention to laughter
Give attention to justice
Give attention to passing days
Give attention to the species
Give attention to the dead

The Jewish Holidays

NITZAVIM/Standing   Deuteronomy 29:9 to 30

30:11-19 Surely, this Instruction that I enjoin upon you is not too baffling for you, nor is it beyond reach. . . . No, the thing is very close to you, in your mouth and in your heart, to observe it. . . . I have put before you life and death, blessing and curse. Choose life — if you and your offspring would live . . .

"Nothing but idolatry, incest, and murder should be allowed to stand in the way of saving a life," says the Talmud (*Yoma* 82a). The preservation of fossil-fuel profits or political power is not included as an excuse for inaction.

Treason

Is it fair to call climate denial a form of treason?
—Paul Krugman

VAYALEKH/And He Went *Deuteronomy 31*

31:1-12 Moses went and spoke these things to all Israel. He said to them: I am now one hundred and twenty years old. I can no longer be active. Moreover, the Lord has said to me, "You shall not go across yonder Jordan." . . . Every seventh year, the year set for remission . . . you shall read this Teaching aloud in the presence of all Israel. Gather the people — men, women, children, and the strangers in your communities — that they may hear and so learn . . .

Moses hands over his power as prophet and leader to Joshua in "Vayalekh." He also completes writing down the Torah, and urges his people to gather every seven years to read it and "observe faithfully . . ." A legend about the death of Moses tell of his soul's reluctance to part from his body, until "God" comes and says, "Daughter, the time of your sojourn in the body of Moses has ended . . ." Then God kisses Moses, and his soul rushes forth in ecstasy.

Funeral

I was at the funeral of Rabbi Devora Bartnoff, in 1997.
She was, possibly, the first woman rabbi ever to die, at least in modern times —
in her forties, a mother of four, and a forthright, wise soul.

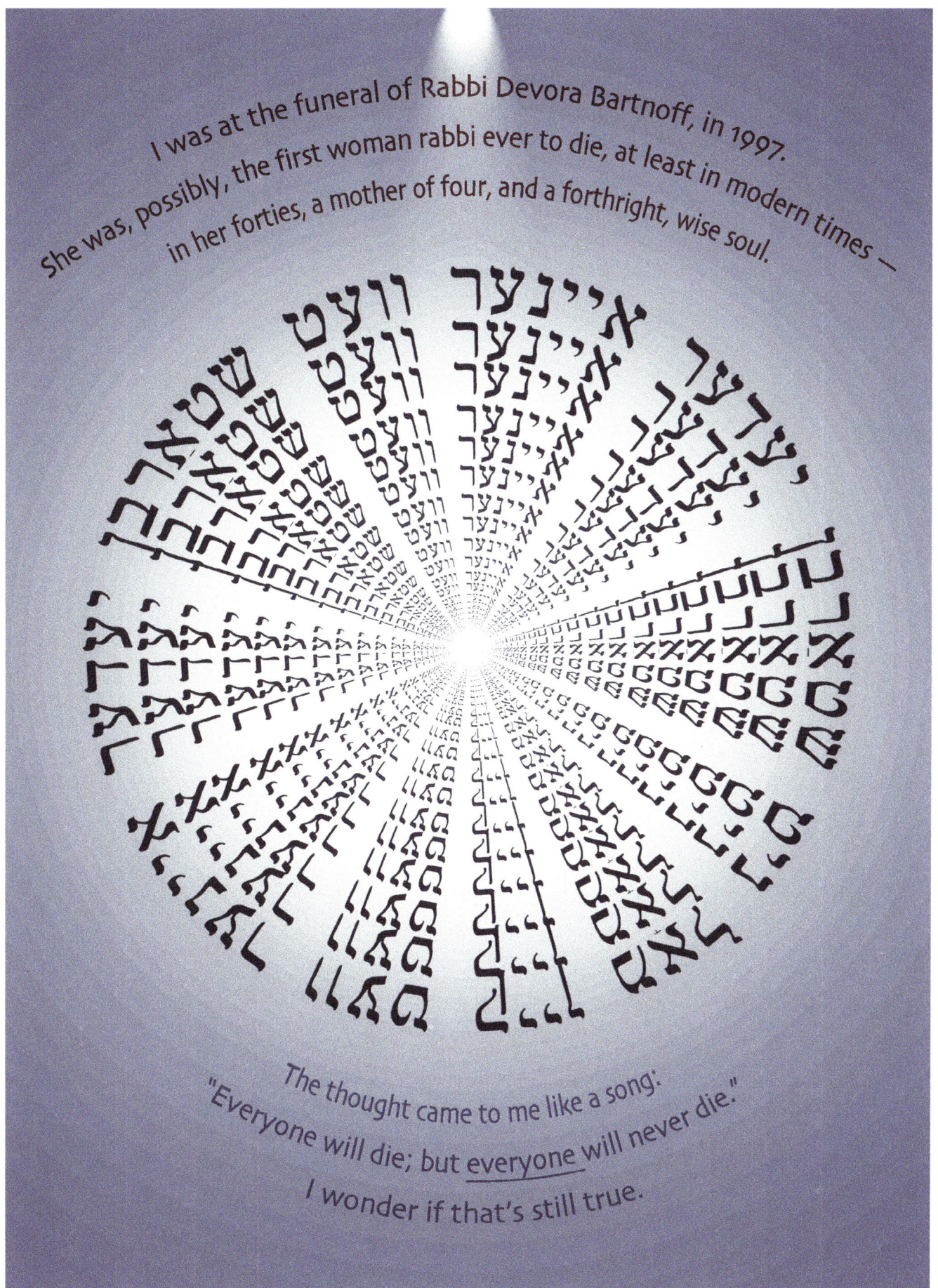

The thought came to me like a song:
"Everyone will die; but <u>everyone</u> will never die."
I wonder if that's still true.

In this Torah portion, "God" shows Moses the mountain, Mount Nebo, on which he will die after gazing down upon the Promised Land.

If I prayed, I would pray at the crack of dawn, as the fog lifted, for the fog to lift for everyone.

Like Droplets on the Grass

V'ZOT HA'BRAKHA/This Is the Blessing
Deuteronomy 33 to 34

33:13-16 With the bounty of dews from heaven,
And of the deep that couches below;
With the bounteous yield of the sun,
And the bounteous crop of the moons;
With the best from the ancient mountains;
And the bounty of hills immemorial;
With the bounty of Earth and its fullness . . .

The Torah concludes with Moses' farewell to the tribes he has led from slavery to peoplehood. He then dies at age 120, and "no one," the Torah declares, "knows his burial place to this day." Leadership has passed to Joshua, who will lead the conquest of Canaan, as detailed in the Book of Joshua, the first of the Bible's books about the prophets, judges, and kings of ancient Israel.

This Is the Blessing

There's so much to buy. What shall we buy? So much to eat. What shall we eat?
So much to see. What shall we see? So much to hear. What shall we hear?
So much to build. What shall we build? So much to protect. What shall we protect?
So much to learn. What shall we learn? So much to forget. What shall we forget?
So much to love. So much to feel. So much to do. What shall we do?

Lawrence Bush's many books include *Pinko Jew*, a collection of artworks and writings from his years editing *Jewish Currents* magazine; *BESSIE: A Novel of Love and Revolution*; *Waiting for God: The Spiritual Explorations of a Reluctant Atheist;* and *American Torah Toons: 54 Illustrated Commentaries*. His essays, fiction, and art have appeared in the *New York Times, MAD magazine, Tikkun, Moment*, the *Forward, The Reconstructionist, Jews.,* and other publications.

Other titles by Lawrence Bush from Ben Yehuda Press

"With courage Bush walks the tightrope between atheism and the temptations of belief. His spiritual peregrinations are deeply personal, searingly honest, wise and witty. Seldom has 'waiting' been so dynamic, fascinating and insightful." — Dr. Joseph Chuman, Columbia University

Waiting for God offers a probing look at the generational factors that led the Woodstock Generation down the path of spirituality. Lawrence Bush grasps, from the perspective of a "reluctant atheist," the sense of ineffable connection that defines contemporary spirituality, and challenges skeptics and humanists to provide spiritual leadership to a hungry age.

"Bush has a reputation for independent and unpretentious thought and dialog. Here, he continues that tradition . . . for both general readers of theology and more seasoned readers looking for a convenient grappling with the issues." —*Library Journal*

"A marvelous story about an amazing woman. It will grip you from beginning to end." —*Hadassah Magazine*

This profoundly optimistic historical novel traces the life of a woman who is a leader in a generation of Jewish fighters and poets. Bessie's "career" as a revolutionary extends from Tsarist Russia to 1960s segregated America, and is filled with hazards, sacrifices, joys and revelations.

"*History is not made like you make a cup of coffee. They say that a Jewish man prayed to God. He said, 'Lord, to you a thousand years is just a minute and a million dollars is like a penny. So please, God, give me a penny?' And God said, 'Wait a minute.'*"

With action-packed chapters that alternate between third- and first-person narratives, BESSIE is a masterful achievement of passion, grace, and wit.